FROM FAIRWAY TO HEAVEN

Dear Claire,

All the best,

April 2021

FROM

FAIRWAY

TO

HEAVEN

Daily Bread for Every Golfer

By

STIRLING

Protestant Version

H³ Books Company

FROM FAIRWAY TO HEAVEN

published by H³ Books Company

Copyright © 2016 by H³ Books Company

Printed by CreateSpace, An Amazon.com Company

ISBN 978-0-9949522-0-2

For more information:

H³ Books

North Vancouver, British Columbia, Canada

info@H3Books.com

For
every golfer on the planet
and
all Christian believers

FOREWORD

HAVE YOU EVER NOTICED THAT it's easiest to talk about God when things are going well in our lives? When we feel showered in blessings, we want to thank God and share with everyone the good news about how He's blessed us. We can come to take God's goodness for granted, almost as if we expect to be blessed. At the beginning of the Book of Job, he is a prosperous man with a good life, a happy family, and thriving business, and he's also a man of strong faith, always praising God and doing everything he must to worship Him. But then the devil is given permission to ruin Job's life and take away all the good things he had. The rest of the Book of Job describes Job's struggle to learn how to praise God when things are going very badly.

I can relate to Job in many ways, except that when my life took a bad turn, it wasn't because the devil had been told he could take away the good things in my life. I was facing the collapse of my family business. It had thrived for over one hundred years, but now, under my watch, it was crumbling. I was extremely distraught. I didn't blame anyone else—not even God—but I did take a long, hard look at the life I was leading. I was not like Job at the beginning of his story. For several years before this collapse, my life had been marked not by faithfulness to God, my family, or my business, but instead was marked by heavy drinking and long hours on the golf course. I had been devoting myself entirely to the wrong pursuits. My drinking and relentless obsession with golf were a formula for disaster, and disaster had struck. All of my priorities were jumbled. God and my family were left behind as I pursued drunkenness and golfing. My business was mixed up in there somewhere, but not a high enough priority for me to save it in time.

As I took stock following the collapse of my family business, I began to blame my time spent on the golf course for my troubles. Don't get me wrong: that didn't stop me from playing every chance I got! But as I needed a place to lay blame, the golfing seemed like the obvious cause of my problems.

Thankfully, although it might be easier to talk about God when our lives seem to be going well and we are enjoying worldly success, God has a tendency to meet us when times are tough. Although we can be close to Him when things are going very well, it is often through suffering that He draws us to Himself and guides us towards wisdom. God met me in my time of hardship and helped me to see the things that had been holding me back from living a good, full life in His Spirit. As I began reflecting—and eventually began praying—about how I had been living my life, I came to realize that golf itself wasn't causing me harm. Golf is just a game. It isn't evil or good—it's neutral. Evil enters in based on our choices. I chose to use golf to escape from my problems. I chose to spend so much of my time and money on the game that my family's century-old business collapsed. Unlike Job, that wasn't taken from me just because the devil wanted to test me. It was taken from me because of my own bad choices. I wasn't devoting enough time to my business, my family, or my faith, and I was devoting far too much time to my golf game. With all the devotion that I have given to golf, I think I might have earned at least one PhD! But God was about to give me something much more valuable than a PhD.

Through the collapse of my business, God helped me to rediscover my faith in Him. He helped me to reorder my priorities, so that He was once again first in my life. The other good things that He had given me could then be put back in their right places as well. God, my family, and a new business venture could become my new priorities. The Lord also helped me to see that golfing wasn't something that I had to give up, but I did need to make sure that I used golf wisely. It made me think about fire: it could be good or bad depending on how we use it. Fire can heat our home or burn it down. As we use it, we must be wise.

After all, God showed me that golf didn't have to be a curse for me. It could be a blessing. Although it is true that my bad decisions and my misuse of golf cost me my business and nearly cost me my family as well, God was good and saved me in the nick of time. I could look back on those years as a waste of time and money, or I could allow God to redeem those years. That's what has led me to write this book. I've come to see that God was not absent even while I was ignoring Him. He has given me insights into the ways that my beloved pastime can teach me about following Him.

I often wonder now if the hardships that I suffered were actually gifts from God, things that I *had* to experience to grow closer to Him. Although it can be easy to talk about God when things are going well in our lives, I don't think I could praise Him nearly so loudly if I hadn't gone through this time of suffering. I am so thankful that He has shown me His wisdom about golf and life and following Jesus, and I am humbled by the opportunity to share those insights with you.

Contents

INTRODUCTION

THIS BOOK ISN'T GOING TO lower your golf score overnight. (Sorry!) The aim of this book isn't to help you play better golf, but to help prepare your head and heart for a round of golf that is good and Godly, even if your scores never change. I hope that it will help you not to feel bad after a bad round and to enjoy your favourite game even more than you already do. Golf can be a great way to learn how to live our lives, and for me it has been a source both of frustration and inspiration that have led me to write this book.

Each of the chapters is based on a reflection that I have had on the golf course or at church about how golf and our walk with God can be similar, or how I think we can learn to be better golfers or better Christians. You will find chapters on golf technique (from a non-technical point-of-view), equipment, etiquette, and history. You will also find reflections on subjects like hope, grace, and faith that are a part of our relationship with God, ourselves, and others. We are all at different places in our walk with God or our level of golfing mastery. This book aims to meet each one of us where we are at, reminding us of things that we already know and challenging us to grow and try new things. I hope that you are able to dip in and find something that will help you on the course and off as you play golf and follow Jesus.

DAY DREAMING

God is spirit, and His worshipers must worship
in the Spirit and in truth.

John 4:24

I WAS ON THE FAIRWAY approaching the twelfth hole on a beautiful summer day. The dew was shining off the grass in the early morning sun. The breeze was gentle and I was feeling great. I took out my six iron, figuring it to be about 170 yards to the flag. I held the club like it was a part of my body. The grip seemed to melt into my hands. It should, after all: I had paid enough money for it! I looked at my line and began my pre-shot routine, then addressed the ball. As I was completing the perfect arc of my swing, I was rudely interrupted.

"God is spirit, and His worshipers must worship in the Spirit and in truth," said the pastor.

The fairway disappeared and was replaced by reality. I was sitting beside my wife in church, supposedly listening to the sermon. The pastor was looking out at the congregation as he spoke. I hoped he hadn't noticed me staring off into space. It wouldn't have been the first time I had done it, though. Every Sunday I came to church, but every Sunday I spent most of the service thinking about my game the day before. I hadn't been worshipping God in spirit and truth. I had been day dreaming about golf. I prayed in church, of course, but mostly just to ask God what was wrong with my game after all the time and money I had invested. Even after going to church for years, I was still trapped in my sins, focused on myself. I should have been asking God about my character, not my golf technique.

But that week as the day dream drifted away, I found myself actually listening to the pastor. His sermon seemed to be speaking to me. I couldn't believe it! As I listened to him, I felt like his sermon was an answer to prayer, since he seemed to be talking about the problems I had in my game. For the first few weeks, I thought it was just my imagination. I tried to ignore my thoughts because they seemed like things I was just making up to make myself feel better. But the things I was hearing didn't really feel like my own thoughts. I've never really been smart enough or holy enough to make the connections that I was thinking about on my own. It's not like I was hearing God dictating and I was just His secretary, writing down the things He was saying. It was more like He was guiding my thoughts and shaping the way that I heard the sermons to show me that in all the time I was spending on the golf course, I had been learning about Him, too.

I started making notes about the ways the sermons related to my golf game. My friends at church probably thought I'd suddenly become quite the holy guy, quietly taking notes on all the sermons. Little did they know I was actually writing down my thoughts about golf! I looked like a man of good faith, but my heart still wasn't pointed in the right direction. Like playing golf, I could "play" at being a good, Church-y Christian. I could start or stop playing at any time.

But God was working on me as I listened to those sermons and took my notes about golf. God knew how much I loved golf and therefore He chose golf to teach me more about loving Him. As I sat in church, God began to show me how to compare golf and following Jesus. The things I was learning about following God from my pastor applied perfectly to golf. But as I thought about it more, I came to realize that many of the lessons I had learned as a golfer also applied to Christianity. God took the things I had learned even while I was sinfully misusing golf and redeemed them to help me to be a better follower of Jesus. Then He encouraged me to share those things I had learned with other people who want to know more about golf and God.

What is Golf?

THE TRUE ORIGINS OF GOLF are lost to time. There are many theories about where and when golf began, though most people agree that Scotland gets to claim the sport as we know it today. It's easy to imagine what the first golf game might have looked like. Two or three young shepherd lads are wandering the heather-covered hills of the Scottish Highlands. They are guiding their sheep with their crooks. (A crook is a long staff with a hook at one end that can be used to rescue fallen animals.) In the afternoon, while the sheep are quietly grazing, the bored shepherds might have started a little game to see how far they could hit a stone using the curved end of their staves. The same tool that is called a comfort in Psalm 23:4 might have been used to begin the game of golf.

When they had finished breakfast, Jesus said to Simon Peter,
"Simon son of John, do you love me more than these?" He said
to him, "Yes, Lord; you know that I love you." Jesus said to him,
"Feed my lambs." A second time he said to him, "Simon son of
John, do you love me?" He said to him, "Yes, Lord; you know
that I love you." Jesus said to him, "Tend my sheep." He said to
him the third time, "Simon son of John, do you love me?" Peter
felt hurt because he said to him the third time, "Do you love
me?" And he said to him, "Lord, you know everything; you
know that I love you." Jesus said to him, "Feed my sheep."

John 21:15-17

Like Simon Peter, all Christians are called to be shepherds. This isn't literal, of course, since there aren't enough actual sheep in the whole world for every Christian to be a shepherd, and I think we would all quickly tire of the taste of mutton. But we are called to have the character of shepherds: to care for one another the way shepherds care for their sheep, to care for creation, and to be humble. Jesus even calls himself a shepherd and King David called God a shepherd in Psalm 23.

In reflecting on how shepherds might have been the first golfers and how we are called to be shepherds, it occurred to me that golf might be the most Biblical game of all. We can look at the things in our life as being either worldly or Godly, unfaithful or faithful, unholy or holy. I used to think that golf was a very worldly, unfaithful, unholy thing. But as I listened to God, I came to see that golf is a very Biblical game in many ways.

Although now we play with clubs instead of crooks and on golf courses instead of on the "lynkes land" of old Scotland, modern golfers and those young shepherds still have a lot in common. Walking a course still immerses us in creation, the way that shepherds spent their time in far pastures surrounded by the beauty of what God has made. Alone in their pursuit, both the shepherd and the golfer are accountable for their own actions. Golfing well calls us to be our best selves and to exercise Christian virtues. Because there is no referee, golf is ultimately a game about conscience, honesty, and integrity.

In 2016, golf will be included for the first time in the summer Olympic Games since 1900. Because of the nature of how golf is played and scored, it will be the only Olympic sport that has no referee. There will be a rule official to help determine questions about the rules, but each player is ultimately responsible for his or her own game. They will need to listen to their conscience, practice honesty, and stand up with integrity about whether or not they have followed the rules, even if it means taking a penalty to their strokes. The Olympic golfers will be helped along by the crowds, their fellow competitors, and the millions of television viewers, but when we head out on the course, often we are the only ones watching our shots. And God, of course.

If we find that we've done something on the course that would cost us a stroke, we have to decide whether or not we mark it on our scorecards. Perhaps we touched the sand in the bunker before we hit the ball. Do we take the penalty or pretend it never happened? If our ball falls behind a tree in the rough, do we "accidentally" knock it out from behind the tree with our foot, or do we make the shot in the wrong direction even though it will mean one or two more strokes on our card? If we want to play golf in a way that honours God, then we have to listen to His Holy Spirit speaking to our consciences. It might cost us the round. But if we are lying to ourselves and before God, isn't the price much higher?

Living with integrity means owning up even when there is a high cost to ourselves. It means acting with honesty according to the rules of golf and the rules of life. There are no referees in our faithfulness to God and His will in our lives. Just like those lonely shepherds, we don't have millions of television viewers holding us accountable to following the rules. God will be our rule official, helping us to interpret the rules correctly through His Word—and ultimately He will decide to give us the "gold medal" or not—but day-to-day we have to be accountable to ourselves. Will our conscience be clean?

We might not know exactly when or where golf began, but we do know that by 1457, golf was popular enough in Scotland to begin to distract people from "more important" activities. Under King James II, the Scottish government ordered that golf be "cried down" as a waste of time. The kingdom preferred that young men practice their archery in case they needed to defend their borders against the English invaders. Kings James III and James IV repeated this ban on golf—especially on Sundays, when archery should be practiced after church—until in 1502 Scotland signed a treaty with England, ending the threat of invasion. Later that year, King James IV himself became the first person in recorded history to purchase a set of golf equipment!

So what makes golf so fun that everyone from shepherds to kings wants to play it? For one thing, golf feels a little bit out of our control, like life itself. We might make plans, learn strategies, or take lessons, but when we get out on the course, there are so many things out of our control that could throw our plans into chaos. A sudden gust of wind could knock our perfectly struck drive right into the rough. Or a fox could run onto the green and steal the ball that was lying just right for a short putt to the hole! We might think we have everything under control, but the game usually has some surprises for us. If golf was easy, then people wouldn't play.

Golf is admittedly a little addictive. Like any good thing, it can be misused, just like I did, trying to escape my problems on the course. But what makes golf addictive is that it drives us to be better. If you play a bad round, you want to get out again, aiming to lower your score next time. You take notes about the mistakes you made so that you can change your swing or your strategy the next time. If you play a good round, you want to play another one just like it, or try to beat that good round with an even better one. Like anything in life, if we want to be good at golf, we need to devote time and energy to improvement.

That's why we need to play with honesty and integrity. If we don't, we won't learn from our mistakes. We will just keep repeating them. The same thing is true in our lives. If we don't own up honestly to the things we've done wrong, we're doomed to repeat them. If we are sinning against God or other people—or even ourselves—then we need to be honest and confess that sin. We need to mark down the bad stroke on our scorecard. That way, when we try again, we can try not to do the wrong thing that caused us to sin in the first place.

SIMILARITIES

WHEN IT STRUCK ME THAT golf was such a Biblical game, I began to consider the similarities between playing golf and following God. There really are a surprising number of things that golf and following God have in common! I will touch on many of these similarities throughout this book, but I wanted to highlight a few here before we go much further.

One of the biggest similarities I've found between golf and following God is that the more knowledge you have about doing it, the harder it becomes to apply. In golf, a person might *know* a lot about how to play the game without actually having the physical skill to apply that knowledge. That's why there are so many golf instructors and so few tour players! Moving from knowledge to application is one of the hardest things in golf, following God, or even life in general. On Sundays, we listen to sermons and are moved by Holy Spirit, but somehow it's still so hard to apply those words throughout the week. Although it is always worth it to learn more about God and His work in the world, all that knowledge can sometimes get in the way of going out and *doing* God's work in the world.

Between that knowledge and our ability to take action is a crowd of "me's" that are trying to compete for my attention. It's easy for our minds to be filled with the voices of all our needs that are trying to become the most important. You might hear about it in golf talk as well: "You aren't playing against the other players; you're playing against yourself." I don't think that's true, though. I think that when we're out there trying to apply the things we've learned, we're playing against the course (or maybe the course designer), but not against *ourselves* or our natural abilities. As we try to play golf or try to do God's work in the world, we have to learn to silence the competing voices that are trying to make us doubt ourselves or fall into sin.

As we follow God and try to do His work in the world—or as we walk the course and try to keep our score low—we have to learn to pace ourselves. I know that I've found faith to be a little like a twinkling star. Sometimes it burns brightly and sometimes dimly. But I think that if it burned brightly all the time, it would burn itself out. Even if we try to burn brightly all the time, the fact is that even the most faithful Christian struggles with sin and even the best golfer will go through a slump. If we want to make those sin-slumps or golf-slumps shorter and less serious, we have to pace ourselves. In golf, when the professionals make a shot from the tee or somewhere on the fairway, they aren't thinking about the next shot during the walk to where the ball lies. They are just thinking about the walk. They pace themselves. If they spend the en-tire round thinking about the next shot, the next putt, the next tee, then they will burn themselves out. Similarly, if we over-think our walk with God, always planning out what we will do next to please Him, we will burn out our faith.

The best golfers are the ones who are consistent. They don't stay too re-laxed, but they don't push too hard, either. They try to maintain a consistent pace. Their pursuit of golf excellence is based on a steady and consistent habit of daily practice. They know that golf is not like riding a bike: you can't just pick it up after years of not doing it. Our walk with God is the same. If we neglect it for years, we won't be able to just pick it up where we left off. We need to keep practicing it and stay consistent in our pace. That said, it is very difficult to be a perfect holy person all the time, and the truth is we cannot do that (certainly not on our own!). If we find ourselves in a golf slump, the only thing we can do to get out of it is to keep practicing. If we find ourselves in a faith slump, then the only thing we can do to get out of it is to keep praying. We need to stay consistent.

We *will* struggle with our faith, just as we will struggle with our golf game. We are being tested all the time. But struggles and tests don't have to be bad things. It is in the struggle that our faith can grow strong. It is when we make bad shots that we learn where the weaknesses are in our swing. And the fact is that we won't really learn from our struggles until we're on the course. We can make beautiful shots at the driving range, straight and long, with a perfect plane, but the trick is learning how to apply what we've been practicing on the range out on the course. The truth is, that will be harder than we think. Listening to sermons, going to Bible studies, and reading Christian books are the same as practicing on the driving range. We have to find a way to apply all the good things we learned to our actual walk with God out there in the real world.

Ultimately, though, we have to learn not to hold too tightly to our walk with God or our golf game. The more we try to control things, the more we will struggle against them. Proverbs 4:27 says "Do not swerve to the right or to the left; turn your foot away from evil." In golf, we want to do the same thing, not overdoing anything—like holding the grip too tightly or overswinging—in case we hook or slice the ball. We have to relax into the grip and let our muscle memory take care of the swing. Trying to control everything will end badly, just as trying to control our walk with God will leave us struggling. We have to try to be faithful, pacing ourselves and learning to apply all the knowledge in our heads to the real world. But we also have to remember what it says in Matthew 26:41: "...the spirit indeed is willing, but the flesh is weak." Just as that is true for our walk with God—that we know the right thing to do but we struggle to do it—it is also true for our golf game. We might *know* exactly what shot we need to make, but it might be too far or too difficult for our physical capabilities.

It might be tempting to aim for perfection, either as a golfer or as a follower of Jesus. But you won't reach perfection in either golf or your life, at least on this side of eternity. Golf is a game of misses—the fewer mistakes you make, the better your score will be. In many ways, being a Jesus-follower is the same thing. We need to work on making fewer mistakes rather than aiming to be perfect. That perfection is the work of the Holy Spirit and is out of our hands. We have to let go of the need to be in control. I heard that the founder of Samsung once said that the only two things he could never achieve was raising his children the way he planned and playing a perfect golf game. I think that sums things up perfectly: we can try our hardest to control our golf game or our faith (or our children), but there are too many things that are out of our hands. We have to give up control.

I've also noticed that golf is a game of opposites. If you want to hit the ball to the left, you have to aim to the right (and vice versa). It doesn't make sense to us at first glance, but the physics of the golf shot just works that way. The secret is that following Jesus is the same: it's a game of opposites. So much of what we are called to do as Christians is opposite of what the world thinks is sensible. Take Matthew 5:38-39, for example: "You have heard that it was said, 'Eye for eye, and tooth for tooth.' But I tell you, do not resist an evil person. If anyone slaps you on the right cheek, turn to them the other cheek also." Most people in our culture would suggest hitting back if you are slapped, but Jesus tells us to let the person who slapped us take a swipe at the other cheek, too. Definitely opposite of what most people would want to do!

Finally, I have found both golf and Christian worship to be places where people come together despite their many differences—even different languages! Golfers around the world all know the rules of the game. There are only small differences between golf course styles around the world. If you golf when you travel, you might find yourself matched with a foursome of strangers who don't speak the same mother tongue. I bet that all of you can communicate about the game, however, since you all know the essentials of what is happening on the course. Christian worship can be the same, just as in Acts 2:1-12. I've been in worship services where there are people from around the world all singing or praying in their own language. I may not have the gift of understanding tongues, but in my spirit I was able to understand that we are all worshipping the same God.

So I hope you can see, like I have, that there are so many similarities between playing golf and following God. This chapter just covered a few of them, but the rest of this book will cover many others. When God showed me these similarities, it helped me to appreciate my golf game more, and it helped me to take the many things I'd learned about golf and use them to be a better follower of Jesus. I still have a long way to go, but I hope that I am still lowering my score. I pray that this book will help you to do that, too.

TRINITY

NOT ALL OF MY REFLECTIONS about the similarities between golfing and following God have been deeply serious. One thing I've noticed is that both Christianity and golf have a thing about trios. Obviously, the most important one is the union of the Father, Son, and Holy Spirit. The "holy trinity" of golf is the physical, mental, and mechanical. Even that can be broken down. The mechanical part can be broken into PGA—not the Professional Golf Association, but what they teach us, which is that PGA stands for Posture, Grip, and Alignment. As we work out the mechanics of our walk with God, we concentrate on prayer, Scripture, and meditation on the Word. In the swing, there's another threesome: tempo, timing, and rhythm. These three things have to be synchronized. You need all three to be the best golfer you can be. 1 Corinthians 13:13 tells us that we need faith, hope, and love. The greatest of the three might be love, but you need all three to be the best Christian you can be. As I kept going through Scripture, I kept seeing the three's: perseverance, character, and hope (Romans 5:3); being joyful, thankful, and prayerful (1 Thessalonians 5:16-18); one Lord, one Faith, one Baptism (Ephesians 4:5). Do some digging yourself and I think you'll find even more trios!

I also noticed that the golf game itself is structured into the long game, the short game, and putting. Our Christian life has three stages as well: justification, sanctification, and glorification. Justification is the understanding that grace is freely given, whether we deserve it or not. It is given to us by a God that really does love us. Sanctification is what we do with the faith that is given us, with the help of the Holy Spirit. And glorification is what comes to us after we die, when we are re-united with God. The great thing about our faith is that it is not us that goes to meet God, rather it is He who meets us.

Application

---

*"Watch and pray so that you will not fall into temptation.
The spirit is willing, but the flesh is weak."*

Matthew 26:41

---

*In the same way, faith by itself,
if it is not accompanied by action, is dead.*

James 2:17

G REG NORMAN ONCE SAID THAT he would be happy if he could make five perfect shots during a round. His standards are certainly much higher than ours for golf, but what about in our walk with God? How often, say, do we make five perfect decisions or actions in the course of an average day? Or maybe we could ask ourselves how many days we follow Scripture closely and act upon its teachings. What kind of score would we get? If we are brutally honest with ourselves, what percentage of our time is actually spent following Scripture? Fifty percent? Five? In his letter in Bible, James reminds us that having faith by itself—without acting on that faith—is useless. Our faith is dead if we aren't acting on it. We won't be able to get a 100% perfect score, but we need to be aiming for "five perfect shots" that demonstrate our faith in Christ.

As I've already mentioned, applying the things we learn from sermons or Bible studies can be incredibly hard. Consider what it's like when you're preparing a swing. You've approached the ball, adjusted your grip, thought about how hard you need to hit the ball, and then you take a practice swing or two. Those practice swings might feel perfect! In your mind's eye, you can see the ball flying straight and far. Then when you finally make the real swing to hit the ball, it's like some kind of animal took over. That animal just wants to kill that ball! The controlled practice swings are a distant memory as the ball pops high in the air and much too far to the right. The same thing happens when we try to go from the "practice swing" in our faith to the real world. Without a real "ball"—a real situation with real people and real temptations—it's easy to picture ourselves living a perfect Christian life. But when we have that real life situation in front of us, sometimes that animal comes out. Maybe the animal is lust or greed or pride (1 John 2:16). It gets in the way and seems to take over so that our beautiful imaginary Christian life goes up in a puff of smoke.

The practice mat at the driving range is very soft and forgiving, but on an actual golf course we have to contend with real grass, hazards, every imaginable kind of lie, and, of course, the rough. Unlike that practice mat, real ground is solid and unforgiving. English and Scottish golfers especially have to deal with diabolical bunkers, deep rough, and unpredictable winds coming off the ocean. Playing under those conditions is much more challenging! It's the same thing for our Christian walk. Being a Christian is so much easier within the comfortable walls of the church, with forgiving brothers and sisters. But life outside the church is much more solid, unforgiving, and unpredictable.

When we're practicing at the driving range or the putting green, we might make some terrific shots and feel really confident about our skills. Then, when we go out to play an actual game, we can end up so disappointed. The amazing shots from practice just aren't coming now. *Where has my game gone?* we might ask. *Why is it so hard to apply what I practice out here on the course?* I've seen many top professionals take that five minute walk from the practice range to the first hole and then make a surprisingly bad shot, even after practicing like a champion minutes earlier. Golf is pretty unforgiving. The shots we make on the practice range don't count when it comes to the real game. Even tennis players get two serves in a real match in case they blow the first serve. But there's no second chance in golf. If you miss that first shot, it counts. In golf, the move from the practice range to the course is almost as serious as moving from practicing your fencing with a foam-tipped foil to dueling with real, deadly blades. That word "to" is so important, whether we're moving from the practice range *to* the first hole or from the church *to* the parking lot. It's a small word with a big impact.

So how do we deal with the little word "to" that creates big space between how we practice and how we perform? For our golf game, it basically comes down to smart practice! We need to create muscle memory so that our body knows exactly what to do to repeat the good shots from the driving range out on the golf course. When our bodies are strong and well-trained in the right way to swing, then we can trust that the muscles will know what to do when we're playing a real game of golf. Our muscle memory becomes the "to" that will carry us from the practice range to the first tee.

In our faith, we have lots of opportunities to train our walk with God—from prayer to listening to wise teachers to reading Scripture—but when those animals come out that make us want to "kill the ball," then we can collapse out there in the real world. So we have to get up again and again, continuing to learn, to pray, and to read. We repent, start over, and try to build our walk back up again. We have to accept that we are broken people, so we *will* find ourselves overwhelmed sometimes. In fact, you'd better understand right now that you can't get this done on your own. Golf and our walk with God have a lot in common, but not this: as we follow Christ, He will give us strength. He gives us grace when we mess up, knowing that our human effort will never be enough on its own.

Golf doesn't have much grace built into it, and when we get out on the course, no one can swing the club but us. There's no golf pro helping us to line up our feet and shoulders and to keep our elbow straight. But in our walk with God we are blessed to have the Holy Spirit who is there to help guide us as we move from what we've learned *to* real actions in the world. The Holy Spirit is the "to" that carries us from the church building into the parking lot, where the "real world" begins. We can trust the Holy Spirit the way that we trust our golfing muscle memory. We have to trust Him or else we might find ourselves sinking beneath all the troubles in this world (Matthew 14:29-31). Application in golf is hard, but by practicing well in our golf game, we can build up the muscle memory that will take us from practice to the real game. Application in our faith is hard, too, but if we trust in the Holy Spirit, He will take us up off our knees and out to do the work of God.

PRACTICE

---

*...we also glory in our sufferings, because we know that
suffering produces perseverance; perseverance, character;
and character, hope. And hope does not put us to shame,
because God's love has been poured out into our hearts
through the Holy Spirit, who has been given to us.*

Romans 5:3-5

THERE'S NO DOUBT ABOUT IT: practicing is hard work. Even when you're practicing for one of your favourite pastimes, like golf, there are going to be times when it's not fun. This is especially true when we're trying to fix a problem or learn a new technique. It takes a lot of repetition to teach our muscles new habits (or unlearn bad habits). But even when practicing feels like suffering, remember that all of that suffering will lead to good things. In this way, golf and our walk with God aren't just similar, but can actually overlap! The suffering we endure as we practice golf can teach us perseverance—the ability to push through difficult times—and make us into better people with stronger character. All of it builds up our ability to hope, which is our ability to trust in the good things that are promised to us in this life and the next.

We should practice our golf skills as if we were playing a real game. I mean that we should practice with purpose, not just repeating drives and putts over and over. If we practice as if we were playing a real game, then when it comes time to play the real game, we'll play the way we practiced. Do you see how that works? If the way we practice makes us really good at playing the driving range, then that's how we'll play the golf course. But they're very different, aren't they? So practice at the range as close to the way you would if you were on the course, and you will develop the skills you need when you get out for the real game.

The same thing applies to our worship. We should worship as if it was the purpose of our entire life. We want to give ourselves up to worshipping God, completely focusing on Him, losing ourselves in prayer, singing, listening to the Word, and serving our brothers and sisters. That way, when we go out of church to live our lives in the world, we will find that our whole life has become worship. We want everything we do—working at our jobs, spending time with our families, serving our neighbours, playing golf, and so on—to be worship of God. What we "practice" on Sunday becomes real from Monday to Saturday.

Practice requires lots of discipline. It means we have to do it even when we don't feel like it. Let's be honest. If we waited until we *felt* like doing anything, we wouldn't get very much done! It's easy to *talk* about practicing, but never get around to doing it. But talking about it won't get results. Jesus even warns us that paying lip service to Him—or just being all talk—won't get us into heaven. It's actions that are needed (Matthew 7:21). Those actions require self-discipline to get started. We need to be like Paul. He wanted to explain to the Christians in Corinth what discipline means for those who follow Jesus:

Everyone who competes in the games goes into strict training. They do it to get a crown that will not last, but we do it to get a crown that will last forever. Therefore I do not run like someone running aimlessly; I do not fight like a boxer beating the air. No, I strike a blow to my body and make it my slave so that after I have preached to others, I myself will not be disqualified for the prize.

1 Corinthians 9:25-27

Paul was called to be a preacher, so he was being held to a very high standard. It's no good for a preacher to preach, "Do as I say, not as I do." Preachers need to lead with their lives as well as their words. But he's also encouraging the Corinthians to hold themselves to high standards. He's encouraging them to be disciplined in their Christian walk so that they can "win the prize" which is eternal life with God.

If we practice our golf with discipline, keeping at it on a regular basis, then we will develop muscle memory. That means that our bodies will remember how to swing the club without us having to think about it every time. Once we take our minds off of positioning our bodies, we can concentrate on strategy and get more enjoyment out of the game. We have to practice to develop this muscle memory because swinging the golf club correctly feels really unnatural to us. At first, it won't be comfortable. We have to make our bodies "our slaves" with regular, purposeful practice that develops the muscle memory for the new technique.

Similarly, we need to develop spiritual "muscle memory" as we follow Jesus. Like Paul says, we don't want to be running about aimlessly or punching at the air while we practice our faith. We need to practice with purpose. We need to have regular periods of prayer, Bible reading, and other spiritual disciplines if we want following Jesus to be second nature. I have found that memorizing Bible verses has helped me to recall words of comfort and instruction from Scripture even in desperate times. Like developing your golf swing, this won't be comfortable or feel natural at first. But with regular, purposeful practice, it will. Jack Nicklaus says practice doesn't make you perfect, perfect practice with purpose makes you perfect! Practicing either golf or your walk with God will not make you a better golfer or a better Christian in one day. It will take a lot of time. If we make mistakes or fail to do better, we don't give up! We have to get back up and return to the practice range or go back to church and keep practicing.

Did you know that your muscle memory will start to fade in only 72 hours? That's why we need to practice as often as we can—at the driving range if possible, or at home if you aren't able to make it to the range. The key is to keep our muscle memory fresh so that our bodies don't forget the good habits that we've formed. As Christians, we also need to keep up with regular practice. Going to church once a week isn't typically enough to help us grow in our faith. We need to pray every day, read the Bible, go to small groups, and serve others throughout the week. That way our spiritual muscles get worked out every day.

We do need to practice well, of course. That's what "practice with purpose" means. We need to know our swing theory and use that to shape how we practice our swing. As Christians we need to know the Scripture and use that to shape how we pray, serve, and worship. Without good theory and purposeful practice, we'll be lost out on the course or in the real world. But when we practice well, we'll find ourselves more confident out on the course. And as Christians, we'll be more confident out in the real world if we've given ourselves a good foundation of practicing prayers and Bible reading.

As I said at the beginning of this chapter, practicing anything is hard work. Whether we're practicing golf or practicing our faith, both require repetition and consistency in practice. Like it says in the Book of Joshua, "Be very strong; be careful to obey all that is written in the Book of the Law of Moses, without turning aside to the right or to the left" (Joshua 23:6) Golfers don't want to develop bad habits that cause them to slice or hook on a regular basis, and Christians don't want to wander off too far from the law of God, either becoming so zealous that we hurt other people or so lazy that we hurt ourselves.

Also, remember that when we don't practice, it will be others that notice first. That's why it's important to have people in your life (or friends you golf with regularly) who can keep you accountable. Sure, we know that we aren't practicing, but if we have good friends or a regular coach, then they will see the changes in our swing. When we aren't praying regularly and our faith begins to weaken, it's likely to be our family at home that notices the changes first, and then our family at church. Like it says in Galatians 6:7, "Do not be deceived: God cannot be mocked. A man reaps what he sows." If you don't practice, you won't be able to play well. If you don't pray often, you'll struggle with sin. It's important to listen to people who ask you if you've been practicing or if you've been praying. That's a wake-up call to remind you to get back to it, and stop complaining that your golf game or your spiritual life are off.

Practice will pay off the most when things get tough. When we need to make a shot under pressure, it's then that our long hours of practicing will help us relax and trust our muscle memory. When our lives get difficult and God seems far away, it is our long hours spent in His Word and listening to His voice in prayer that will remind us that He will never abandon us. Practicing is hard work and requires discipline, but it pays off so much when we need it most. Like Job says, "But he knows the way that I take; when he has tested me, I will come forth as gold" (Job 23:10). If we're strengthened by practice or prayer, then when we're tested under pressure, we'll shine like gold. So find time in your day for golf and for God, even when you don't feel like it. You will grow as a person and as a golfer, and you'll rest easier knowing that when the game or life gets hard, you will have developed good habits that will strengthen you for the challenge.

SWING

Therefore put on the full armor of God,
so that when the day of evil comes,
you may be able to stand your ground,
and after you have done everything, to stand.
Stand firm then, with the belt of truth buckled around
your waist, with the breastplate of righteousness
in place, and with your feet fitted with the readiness that
comes from the gospel of peace. In addition to all this,
take up the shield of faith, with which you can
extinguish all the flaming arrows of the evil one.
Take the helmet of salvation and the sword of the Spirit,
which is the word of God.

Ephesians 6:13-17

YOU CAN TELL THAT I love golf, because when I read the Scripture passage above, I think about a golfer preparing to swing instead of a soldier wearing armour. I think if Paul had been a golfer, he would have started with the feet and moved upward, but sadly golf had not been invented when he was writing this letter to the Ephesians. But what Paul is talking about is being prepared, and I think that there's a lot in common between the metaphor of a soldier preparing for battle and a golfer preparing to swing. Because the swing is so central to our golf game, I also think there are other ways that we can think about it that help us to think about being followers of Jesus, too.

Like I said, I think that a golf version of this passage would start with the feet. Golfers know that a strong swing starts with having your feet strongly planted, supporting your whole body and providing the foundation of the simple-but-complex maneuver you're about to attempt. We swing from the ground up. Then we could move up to the belt of truth. We want the angle at our waist to stay constant, like truth is constant. Miss out on that and your swing will collapse. Keep your shoulders aligned and breathe comfortably, like putting the breastplate of righteousness in place. Next, Golfer Paul might mention the helmet of salvation. Every golfer knows you have to keep your head stationary. If the helmet represents our salvation, then our stationary head represents making Jesus the centre of our lives. That centre needs to remain fixed in place. Even Jack Nicklaus' instructor, Jack Grout, sometimes had to hold his head in place by the hair while he practiced! When we have second-thoughts or doubts about our swing and we peek up to see where the ball is going to go, what happens? All of our alignment gets skewed and we mess up the shot. It's a bit like Peter peeking at the wind when he was walking out on the water instead of keeping his eyes on Jesus (Matthew 14:30). If we focus on the cross—that is, if we keep our eyes on the ball for as long as possible as we swing—then our lives, like the ball, will go where they need to go.

Finally, the soldier in Paul's metaphor takes up a sword and shield. Golfer Paul would liken that shield of faith to the trust that we have in our swing. We keep our head in place with the helmet of salvation and the shield of faith gives us the protection we need to keep our eyes on the ball, because we trust our swing to do what it should. That will protect us from sending the ball off in any wild direction. The shield acts to blinker our vision, like a race horse. We can focus in on where we've visualized our shot going and not be distracted by the many dangers on the way there. If we drop our shield, our eyes might be distracted by the water hazard on the left or the sand trap on the right and then we'll swing to avoid those things and wind up overcompensating. When we dropped our shield, we lost our trust in our swing and visualization. It isn't enough to minimize our losses. Swing to win and trust your swing.

Last but not least, the sword of the spirit is, of course, like the golf club itself. Brandel Chamblee of the Golf Channel has even compared Tiger Woods wielding his irons to William Wallace, the great Scottish freedom fighter, wielding his sword! The golf club is the spirit of the swing. Without it, we'd look pretty foolish, wind-milling our arms back and forth for no reason. The club delivers on all our other preparations. Our armour will protect us and build up our swing, and the sword—the club—is the tool that we use to make all of that preparation a reality. But remember that the club itself is *just* a tool. Buying a different or more expensive club won't fix a problem in your swing. When my son was in elementary school, he asked for a new pencil, so I gave him one that I'd brought home from the golf course. Naturally, golf pencils are a lot shorter than the pencils most of the other students were using. But did that mean that my son was going to get worse grades than those kids? Of course not! It was hard work and time studying that would change his grades, not the pencil that he used. A new piece of equipment wasn't going to make him a straight-A student, just as a new piece of golf equipment won't make us swing better. We have to fix the faults in our swing first, and then we will probably find most equipment will do the job for us.

There will come a time, though, when we face trouble in our swing. We feel like we've lost our helmet, dented our shield, dulled our sword, loosened our belt, or put our shoes on backwards. What happened to our swing? The only thing we can do now is to put our armour back on the right way. Start back at the basics: posture, grip, alignment, ball placement, and stance. Have you noticed that this metaphor applies to our life as well (just the way Paul intended it in the first place)? When things go nuts in our lives, we need to go back to the basics there as well. Start reading the Bible, and start at the beginning. The Bible tells the story of God's relationship with the universe He created and the people He made to take care of it. If we start at the beginning of the story, in Genesis, we can see that story unfold from beginning to end and it will help us build up a strong foundation for our faith in God.

As we build up our swing, we have to remember that we can only swing our way. What I mean is, we will never be able to swing like anyone else. Even Arnold Palmer said that there's no point in trying to copycat anyone else's swing. Every human being has a unique body, so every human being will have a unique swing. We can all learn the theory of a good swing, but it's up to us (and our instructors) to figure out how to make that work for our bodies. Paul wrote, "to each one of us grace has been given as Christ apportioned it." (Ephesians 4:7) What he means is that each one of us was given different gifts or talents. That means that some of us will be able to hit the ball a long way, others will have pinpoint accuracy, and still others will be able to curve the ball in any direction they wish, like Bubba. We all want a little of each gift, but honestly some of us will be better at each part than the others, and that's okay. Think of it like Christian denominations: there are lots of different kinds of churches now, each one emphasizing a slightly different part of the Christian faith. That's okay. We're all playing the same game—or a Paul might say, running the same race—so it's not a big deal if we all have different swings.

That said, we do have to be smart about the differences between swings, sometimes. In his second letter to Timothy, Paul warns the younger man to watch out for people who have the "form of Godliness" but "deny its power"

(2 Timothy 3:5). What he means is that something a church or Christian is doing might look Godly, but in truth the power of God is not with them. I'm sure we've all met people who call themselves Christians and even act in a way that seems very holy, but later it comes out that they've really been sinning and denying the power of God in their lives for years. The old saying is that the proof of the pudding is in the eating. For a golf swing, the proof is in the power with which we hit the ball. A swing might look great to a spectator, but then the ball goes nowhere (or nowhere good, at any rate). A swing needs to be developed in sequence if it's going to be loaded with power. If there's no sequence in the back swing, there will be no power in the shot. Sometimes it's the people with unorthodox-looking swings that win the tournaments. Their swings might have been "ugly" but they proved their worth with winning shots. The beautiful but badly sequenced swings didn't have what it takes.

How do we sequence our backswing to create the power we need to deliver a good shot? (In other words, how do we set up our lives so that we're not just showing the "form of Godliness" while "denying its power"?) First we need to have a strong takeaway in our swing. As we bring the club back to nine o'clock, we are developing the swing plane that will control the rest of the backswing. In our lives, the "takeaway" period is the repentance period. As we "bring the club up" we realize we are caught in our sins and as we draw the club back, we are repenting and seeking to get right with God. After that strong takeaway, you're on the correct swing plane. The club comes all the way back to the top of the swing, through our period of sanctification—becoming more holy—and then our downswing is the triumphant feeling of glorification—becoming more like God. All of that swing is leading up to the moment of truth.

The last thing I wanted to mention about our swing is that we never want to deliver 100% of our power all the time. You'll notice that the pros manage to withhold probably about 20% on most swings. That way, they know that *if* they need it, they have about 20% more power available to really wallop the ball when necessary. But swinging with only 80% power doesn't make them weak or mean that they're tired. What it means is that they're swinging *gently*. Interestingly, Paul encourages us to show *gentleness* as one of the fruit of the Spirit (Galatians 5:22). Swinging gently (or acting with gentleness) doesn't mean you're out of power. It means you're withholding your strength. It takes a great deal of self-control (another one of the fruits of the Spirit) to do that!

So whether you're developing your golf swing or building up your life in Christ, remember to be prepared, to stay in control, to concentrate on your backswing, and to trust in God. Keep consistent, swinging with the same tempo and rhythm wherever you find yourself. Worship God consistently in every situation. He's there to help you with your life, and, I believe, with your actual golf swing!

VISUALIZATION

Faith is confidence in what we hope for and
assurance about what we do not see.

Hebrews 11:1

GOLF SHOULD NEVER BE LIKE hitting a piñata. We don't swing the club at the ball wildly, hoping we hit it and that it goes somewhere good. One of the most important skills that a golfer needs to learn is the ability to visualize a shot before making it. Golfers need to be able to create a mental image of how they want the ball to go and use that visualization to execute the drive, chip, or putt. The most skilled players are the ones who are able to match up their execution with their visualization with a high degree of accuracy. The golf legend Jack Nicklaus was a genius at this. The idea of visualization has a lot of personal importance to me; my company's slogan was "From vision to reality." It takes a lot of faith to trust in something that isn't yet a reality. Golfers have to practice believing in something that they haven't physically produced yet.

You've probably picked up on the connection between visualization in golf and visualization in our walk with God. We can't see God. Jesus has already ascended to heaven, so unlike Thomas the apostle, we don't get to touch His wounds and see that He is actually alive (John 20:27-28). We just have to have faith. We visualize what heaven will be like, what Jesus is like. With that visualization in our minds, we can execute our life in faith. We can aim for heaven. We trust the outcome and we swing for it.

Trusting your visualization is the second-most important step after the visualization itself. You can't second-guess your visualization or you risk losing it completely. You trust your visualization and then rely on your hand-eye coordination to execute the shot. You develop that hand-eye coordination through many hours of practicing. As a Christian, you develop the ability to live according to God's will for your life after many hours of reading His word and spending time in prayer and worship. That preparation gives us the ability to move from vision to reality. But if we don't trust our visualization—if we second-guess ourselves—then we won't be able to deliver on it. It's like when Peter tried to walk on the water with Jesus (Matthew 14:28-31). He did great so long as he kept his eyes on Jesus, but when he looked down at the water, he became frightened and began to sink. He stopped trusting Jesus and began doubting that it was possible to walk on water. When he started to doubt, his doubts came true and he began to sink. He stopped trusting the visualization he had made of walking on the water towards Jesus.

We also need to visualize the *right* shot. If we use the wrong visualization, we will make the wrong shot and then our ball could end up anywhere. We have to have the right "eye" for things. The world will tell us we need "the eye of the tiger" or "hungry eyes" to see what we want. But as Christians we need to look through the eyes of faith at what we cannot see with our eyes of flesh. We're not trying to be viciously ambitious—having the eye of a tiger—or full of hunger. We trust in things that cannot be achieved or eaten or desired by our flesh. If we want to have a trustworthy visualization, we need to look in

Scripture and listen to the Holy Spirit for guidance. If we don't, I think we could end up like Lot's wife. Everyone was told not to look back at the destruction of the city, but Lot's wife doubted and second-guessed God's command and looked back. Sadly, the result for her was that she became frozen as a pillar of salt (Genesis 19:15-26). We don't want to freeze up on the golf course or in life.

So we need to practice visualization and we need to trust in our visualization. It will benefit us in golf and in life. In golf we can rely on muscle memory and hand-eye coordination to help us to execute our visualization. In life we can rely on our relationship with God and the guidance of the Holy Spirit to help us move from vision to reality as we grow more and more like Jesus.

MOMENT OF TRUTH

"But what about you?" he asked.
"Who do you say I am?" Simon Peter answered,
"You are the Messiah, the Son of the living God."

Matthew 16:15-16

And I saw the dead, great and small,
standing before the throne, and books were
opened. Another book was opened, which is the
book of life. The dead were judged according to
what they had done as recorded in the books.
The sea gave up the dead that were in it,
and death and Hades gave up the dead that
were in them, and each person was judged
according to what they had done.

Revelation 20:12-13

I T'S INCREDIBLE HOW IMPORTANT THAT one moment is. Everything you've invested in your golf game—time practicing, money on clubs and lessons— comes down to the split-second when the club contacts the ball. It's the moment of truth—the impact—when the trajectory, curvature, and speed of the ball are decided. Everything you did leading up to that moment and everything you will do after that moment stop mattering. All that matters is the impact when the metal meets the urethane: the moment of truth. Have you ever noticed that the touring professionals often have different-looking swings, but all hit on the sweet spot? Your swing might be flat, perfect, ugly, beautiful, upright—all of that is forgotten in the moment of truth. Certainly your swing is important, but by itself it's just whistling through the air. You'll know if it was worth it in the moment of truth.

We face two important moments of truth in our lives. First, we have to decide whether we believe, like Simon Peter, that Jesus is the Messiah, the Son of the living God, or not. That moment of truth leads decisively to the final moment of truth. We are preparing for a moment when we will find out where eternity will be spent: in the eternal presence of God or away from Him. It's Judgment Day, when Jesus will judge the living and the dead, and if we are not standing with Him on that day, then we are destined to stand away from Him. Our "swing" may or may not matter; that is to say, the time we spent in church or reading the Bible can help us to line up our lives for the moment of truth, but they aren't all that matters. Just like in golf, we are trying to hit the sweet spot. Without Jesus, that will be impossible.

We have to avoid shanking the ball. Have you ever noticed that shanking is contagious? Once someone in your group shanks the ball, there seems to be more people shanking it after them. Although we're ultimately only responsible for our own shot, we do have an influence on other people, and they can influence us. We don't want to shank the ball and cause others to get nervous so they shank their shots as well. Likewise, if someone's having a bad time and shanks their ball, we don't want to let their bad shot cause us to make the same mistake. I'm sure you can guess what a shank is in the moment of truth in our lives. It means that our lives are sailing off far away from Jesus. We want to aim for a pure impact so that our shot flies straight and true.

GAME PLAN

"...while they were on their way to buy the oil,
the bridegroom arrived. The virgins who were ready
went in with him to the wedding banquet.
And the door was shut.
Later the others also came. 'Lord, Lord,'
they said, 'open the door for us!' But he replied,
'Truly I tell you, I don't know you.'
Therefore keep watch, because you do not
know the day or the hour."

Matthew 25:10-13

THE FAMOUS CREDIT CARD COMMERCIAL asks, "What's in *your* wallet?" The golfer should be asking, "What's in my golf bag? Am I prepared for the course I'm about to play, or is my bag still loaded with clubs from the last course I was on?" As you prepare for your next golf game, you learn about the course where you'll be playing and prepare your bag accordingly. Remember when you were a high school student? Did you ever study math the night before a history test? Of course not! You'd study history before the history test. The same is true for golf preparation. You want to make sure your bag is loaded with the clubs that will serve you best on the specific course you'll be playing on. You might need to pull out that four iron and leave it at home, putting your hybrid club in its place. Maybe you're playing a course that's short-game heavy so you leave the long iron and add another wedge. You only have fourteen slots to fill, so you want to prepare wisely.

In the parable at the beginning of this chapter, Jesus tells the story of the five wise virgins and the five foolish virgins. The wise ones were prepared to wait for as long as necessary for the bridegroom, so they brought extra oil for their lamps. The foolish ones didn't think ahead; they burned up all their oil at the beginning of the night and then had to run to the shops at the last minute, hoping to get back in time. They weren't in time and were locked out of the wedding feast. We learn from that parable to be prepared, since, as Jesus says, we don't know the day or the hour when He will return.

Just as in golf, we need a game plan in life. What course are we preparing for? Do we hope for eternal life with God but we're preparing our "golf bag" for hell instead? Are we loading up with "good deed drivers" or "sin sand wedges"? If we need to know how to prepare our game plan for living a life with heaven as our goal, then we need to study the "course." The Bible is our manual and our course description. It shows us how to live—and not to live—if we want to join Jesus in eternal life. By studying the Bible, we can learn how to prepare ourselves wisely, making sure that we're not one of the foolish virgins who tries to run out at the last minute to get what we need.

Part of our preparation in golf and in life is knowing when to rest so that our bodies and minds are ready for what lies ahead. All of the virgins became drowsy and fell asleep. But I'm betting the wise ones fell asleep easily, knowing that they had extra oil for when the bridegroom came. Are you someone who lies awake at night worrying about the next day's game (or just the next day)? In Matthew 6:33-34, Jesus says, "But seek first his kingdom and his righteousness, and all these things will be given to you as well. Therefore do not worry about tomorrow, for tomorrow will worry about itself. Each day has enough trouble of its own." If we are prepared for heaven because we have been seeking the kingdom and God's righteousness, then we can go to sleep and not worry about the next day. If we've prepped our clubs that night, we can sleep easily knowing that we're ready to drive to the course in the morning. So, what's in *your* golf bag?

INSTRUCTION

Consequently, faith comes from hearing the message,
and the message is heard through the word about Christ.

Romans 10:17

I am writing this not to shame you but to warn you
as my dear children. Even if you had ten thousand guardians
in Christ, you do not have many fathers, for in Christ Jesus
I became your father through the gospel.
Therefore I urge you to imitate me.

1 Corinthians 4:14-16

I T'S SAID THAT YOU SHOULD never teach your spouse or your children either how to drive or how to play golf. It's certainly not something I would recommend except to folks who are very, very patient. Teaching someone how to golf can be a bit like trying to control your own heartbeat. You can expend a lot of effort, but you might only see a little change. Golf instructors are very valuable people, though, since golf is almost impossible to learn by yourself for one simple reason: you can't see yourself swing. Sure, you could make a video of your swing and then try to analyse it, but it will be hard to tell where you're going wrong and you might not know what to do about it.

Instructors are experts in teaching other people. They are trained to see what is going wrong in someone else's swing. Even touring professionals rely on instructors to help them fix bad habits that creep into their swing. It's a funny thing, isn't it? The touring pro plays better than their instructor, but they need that instructor to help them see their swing faults. Good instructors have eagle eyes for seeing little things that we're doing wrong or the places that we could improve. There are lots of people out there who have tips about our golf skills—magazine writers, television hosts, book writers (like yours truly), and even our buddies—but we will really benefit from having only one or two valued instructors who can focus in on helping us play better.

That's sort of what Paul was getting at in the quote from 1 Corinthians 4 at the beginning of this chapter. There are lots of people in our lives who have a voice about our faith—magazine writers, television hosts, book writers, our pastors, and even our friends—but if we really want to grow deeply in discipleship, it helps to have a mentor. This is usually a trustworthy Christian who's a little more mature in their faith than you are. Paul might call that person a "father" in the faith. Mentors work with us one-on-one to help us see where we can become more faithful followers of Jesus. They have a better eye to see where we need to strengthen our faith than we do.

Even if you haven't found a mentor yet, it's important to make sure you're involved in your church community. We are all responsible for helping one another to be better followers of Jesus. God intended us to be in community with one another, like a family. It's very hard to be objective about our own sins sometimes. Our pastors and our brothers and sisters in Jesus are there to guide us gently back to the right path. If we try to go it alone, we run the risk of wandering off a long way. We might start interpreting the Bible only the way we want to, without checking to see if anyone agrees with us. That's a very steep, slippery slope into a pit of sin. That's why we need other people to pull us back whenever we get too close to the edge. And no matter how we might look to the wider world, the people closest to us—our family at home, our friends, and our church family—often see us as we really are. It's harder to hide our sins and failings from them.

I want to share one word of warning, though. It's possible to fall in with a bad mentor or a bad church. Having a mentor isn't helpful if they're teaching us the wrong things. This can happen in golf as well: we think we've found a good instructor, but they teach us techniques that just lead to bad habits, maybe even causing us to injure ourselves. Look for certified instructors because the organization that certified them will vouch for them. Not all spiritual leaders are trustworthy people, either, and many of them just want to manipulate and control others. Listen to people you already trust before committing yourself to being mentored or before joining a new church, and do some research about their denomination.

Having a good instructor will help you to become a better, stronger golfer. Having a good mentor will help you to become a more faithful, more disciplined Christian. Beware of people who are only in it for the money or the power, but don't let the fact that there are a few bad sheep scare you off from getting good instruction. You can't teach yourself to be a great golfer and you can't teach yourself to be a better Christian. Both golf and Christianity are meant to be shared with other people who are all learning to do better together. Finally, please don't expect results overnight. I know how hard it is to wait for things to happen in this fast-paced world, but developing skills in golf or deepening our walk with God take time. Think of it as watching a plant bear fruit. It takes a long time for the plant to grow, produce a flower, and then start growing a fruit, and then you need to wait for the fruit to ripen. It's worth the wait, though, whether you're learning to become a stronger golfer or a more mature follower of Jesus. Be patient with yourself and keep at it!

GOLF SCHOOL

Instruct the wise and they will be wiser still;
teach the righteous and they will add to their learning.
The fear of the Lord is the beginning of wisdom,
and knowledge of the Holy One is understanding.

Proverbs 9:9-10

I RECOMMEND GOING TO GOLF school if you have the chance. It's a very intensive time to learn as much as you can about golf in the company of other people. It won't lower your score that much—and certainly not overnight—but it will give you good advice for improving your play-style and lots of general knowledge about the game. There aren't any short-cuts, though. You still need to practice what you've learned and keep playing the game.

I compare golf school to going to church. Being a part of a church is very important to our walk with God, but just going to church won't make our problems disappear (at least not overnight). Just as going to golf school will widen your perspective on the game, going to church regularly will help you widen your perspective about God and His love for the world He made.

A good golf instructor at a golf school will teach you how to apply swing theory to your actual swing so that you will see results on the golf course. They will teach you the skills you need to find and fix your faults on your own. A good pastor is sort of the same. They give sermons that teach you how to apply the Bible to your actual life so that you will see results in the real world. They teach you how to take what you've learned from your head to your hands. Truth be told, sometimes instructors and pastors only give bandage solutions to our problems that don't get at the root cause of what's going wrong in our swing or our life. So although their teaching is important and helpful, you have to remember that it's still up to you to do the hard work of practicing and praying.

One more thing I've noticed is how many would-be instructors or pastors there are out there. That's why going to a certified golf school or to a church that's part of a well-established denomination are the safest bets. I've noticed that YouTube is packed with videos of people sharing this or that new swing theory. They want to be the founder of some amazing new swing. But it isn't enough just to make something up and then put it out there for other people to try. Proven methods are still used because they still work. The same thing is true for religious things we find on YouTube and other places on the web. Don't trust everything you see or read. The person in the video or who wrote the blog might just be trying to be the founder of a new church for the power. I'm not saying that's always the case; as the Bible says, "Do not quench the Spirit. Do not treat prophecies with contempt but *test them all*; hold on to what is good, reject every kind of evil" (1 Thessalonians 5:19-22, my emphasis). Compare the things you read and hear on the Internet (or anywhere else) to see if they match up with what the Bible says, what Christian tradition says, what your pastor and church say, and what the Holy Spirit is telling you.

FAITH

But when he saw the wind, he was afraid and,
beginning to sink, cried out, "Lord, save me!"
Immediately Jesus reached out his hand and caught him.
"You of little faith," he said, "why did you doubt?"
And when they climbed into the boat, the wind died down.

Matthew 14:30-32

WHAT DOES IT MEAN TO "have faith"? When we say we "have faith" does that just mean that we follow a specific religion like Christianity or Islam or Buddhism? Or does it mean something deeper than that? You've probably already guessed that I think it's something deeper than just calling yourself a Christian (or Muslim or Buddhist). At the heart of faith is trust. Having trust is like having a post-dated cheque. You can't see the actual money that it represents, but you know that it does have value. When we trust someone, we allow ourselves to accept their authority and to do what they say. Golfers do this all the time. Because it's so hard to teach yourself to golf (since you can't see yourself swing), golfers have to trust someone like an instructor or friend to help them learn and improve. We accept the authority of the instructor because we trust them, and we follow their instructions. We know that they can see things in our swing that we are simply unable to see. We *have faith* that the instructor is not going to lie to us or deliberately teach us to swing badly.

I'll be frank: if I approach the Bible from a "scientific" or "rational" point-of-view, then I can struggle to believe what it says. There are lots of instances in the Bible that seem impossible to believe now that we have so much scientific knowledge. But because I have faith in God and believe that He would not lie to me or deliberately teach me to do wrong, I can trust and believe what I read in the Bible. I know that the Bible is like a manual for what it means to be a Godly person. It is full of stories and instructions that help us make right decisions in our lives. Without it, we really have no guidelines for what it means to be a Jesus-follower. So I choose to have faith and to trust that what God has inspired men to write is true and good for me.

HOPE

I T'S ALWAYS EXCITING TO SEE really talented golfers going neck and neck in the last holes of a tournament. I remember a Sunday when a new young player was one shot behind the other leaders when he found himself in the bunker on the last hole. He knew that he needed to hole out that bunker shot if he wanted to join the playoff with the other leaders. That bunker shot was his last hope. When he stepped into the sand that Sunday, he was holding onto that hope as if his very life depended on it.

Hope is a strange word. I think over the years most people have come to use it more-or-less the same way they use the word "wish." As in "I *hope* Mom buys me a new golf bag for Christmas." Unless you have a strong reason to believe that your mom will buy that golf bag, then the correct word to use is "wish." But if you told your mom that you wanted a golf bag, and what bags are best, and where to buy them, then "hope" probably is the right word. The golfer that Sunday had hope because he knew that his skill was high enough to make that shot out of the bunker. He didn't just close his eyes and wish upon a star. He visualized the shot he needed to make and held onto the hope that he could make it. (He did, by the way, and won the tournament on the fifth playoff hole!)

Hope in golf is sadly no guarantee. Like that golfer, you might have every reason to believe that you will win, but then some random thing happens that ruins your putt, or it turns out that your opponent is simply more talented—or luckier that day—than you are. But followers of Jesus have a hope that isn't going to be ruined by chance or stolen away by someone else who's "more deserving." Christians have a hope that is "stored up in heaven" where it is safe and secure and guaranteed. Knowing that God has prepared a place for us—and that His plan is to make the whole universe as wonderful as that place—gives us the security to act out in faith and love because our hope is to be with God in heaven (and someday, heaven-on-earth). Whenever I hear the beginning of that famous song, "Imagine there's no heaven," I shudder. When I imagine there's no heaven, it makes me wonder what the point would be in doing anything here on earth. My hope in heaven drives me and helps me to live life like one of those golfers, always pushing harder to achieve the goal. That goal is eternal life in the presence of God and the company of other Jesus followers.

I think it's important to hope that there is a goal. Remember: that's not *wishing* there is a goal, it's *hoping*, acting in the knowledge that heaven exists. If we live in the hope that is stored up in heaven, then we are empowered to keep going. Life can be such a struggle sometimes, but if we have hope in heaven, then we will have the drive to push through the struggles. Remember the young golfer I mentioned at the beginning of this chapter? He relied on his hope that he could still win the tournament to focus his mind so that he could make that incredible shot from the bunker.

If you find your hope fading, look to the Word of God. The Bible is full of stories of hope and the promises of abundant life in God. That's where you'll find the drive to keep going and the security of knowing that your goal is not just wishful thinking. Keep fighting for the goal knowing that there's always one shot left, and that might be the winning one.

Love

---

*And now these three remain: faith, hope and
love. But the greatest of these is love.*

1 Corinthians 13:13

WHY DO PEOPLE GET MARRIED? (I know that seems off topic for a
book about golf, but bear with me.) I'd argue that people get
married because they love each other *so much* that they want to
make a lifelong commitment to one another. The same thing is true when we
commit our lives to following Jesus at baptism or confirmation. We are saying
that we love Jesus *so much* that we want to spend our lives doing His will and
trying to be more like Him. I think one of the most important characteristics
of love is that commitment. When we love someone or something, we commit
our time, energy, and money to that person or thing.

Have you figured out how this related to golf yet? I think that there's a
big difference between liking golf and loving golf, and that difference is the
commitment we make to the game. A part of that commitment is sacrifice.
Really, when we give our time, energy, and money to the game, we are sacrific-
ing them. The same is true in marriage or in our faith. I hear people saying,

"I love such-and-such" all the time, but I don't think that's what they mean. It's obvious that they aren't ready to sacrifice time, energy, and money to that thing or person. They mean that they *like* it. If we genuinely love someone or something, we will suffer for them if needed. If we only *like* someone we are unlikely to endure hardship on their behalf.

Love is required for the kind of devotion that fuels excellence. We need to be ready to make sacrifices if we want to get better at golf or at following Jesus or in our relationships. If we only like something, we probably won't have that kind of devotion. So we need to ask ourselves, "how much do I love this/them?" I think we'll find that our level of love is reflected in how hard it is to make the sacrifice or time, energy, or money. If we struggle to make the time to practice golf or pray to God, then we might need to check our love level.

Before I go further, I want to make one thing clear: like many people have said, love is a verb. Sure, we have feelings around love, but those feelings don't mean anything if we don't act on them. So if we want to grow our love level, we need to start acting in love. If we want to grow more in love with Jesus, we need to take time to pray and read the Bible. If we want to grow our love of golf, we need to practice and spend time on the course. If we want to grow our love of people, we need to do things for them, spend time with them, and listen to them. In 1 Thessalonians 1:3, Paul writes, "We remember before our God and Father your work produced by faith, *your labour prompted by love*, and your endurance inspired by hope in our Lord Jesus Christ" (my emphasis). Love does take labour, but when we love something, that labour doesn't seem quite as hard.

Love will help us labour through a lot of things. Had a bad round? It probably isn't *quite* as frustrating if you love golf. Spending most of your weekend at church or serving in volunteer positions? It's not as hard when you love Jesus. Getting up at 6am on Saturday to get your kid to the rink for practice? If you love your child, it's not such a struggle. So check your love levels and decide where you can grow them. Act in love and your love will grow. The more you love, the easier it is to keep loving. It's a wonderful cycle!

HONESTY

I have fought the good fight,
I have finished the race,
I have kept the faith.

2 Timothy 4:7

ONE OF THE FIRST MORAL lessons we have to teach a child is that they should tell the truth. Because we are such broken, sinful creatures, it seems that children learn to lie almost at the same time that they learn to speak! Dishonesty and cheating are sins that we will all struggle with throughout our lives. It's often easy to justify telling a lie or doing something dishonest. We say that we told a "white lie" or we wonder if it's really dishonest if no one catches us and no one gets hurt. As adults, we have to navigate a world where our words and actions have many consequences and we want to do our best to love God and love our neighbours. But as the old saying goes, honesty really is the best policy in almost all cases.

Golf often offers us the temptation to dishonesty. Although we usually play in groups, the group doesn't necessarily follow us everywhere as we play our ball. Sometimes we might find ourselves alone and in a position where we could improve our score by improving our lie. A little nudge with our toe to move the ball out of a divot or into a clear spot in the rough could make the difference between par and double-bogey. No one is watching. No one will see. Golf has no referees standing on the sidelines watching my every move.

But Someone is watching. We might be able to hide our dishonest actions from our foursome, but we won't be able to hide them from God. Even though no one else will know that we cheated, He will be disappointed that we did something dishonest. Even a "little sin" like cheating creates a brokenness in our relationship with God. Has anyone ever told you a lie and then you found out about it? Perhaps your children, your spouse, or your friends? How did you feel? I bet you felt hurt, betrayed, angry, or sad that this person you trusted and cared for did something dishonest. God has feelings like that, too! When we cheat—even though it isn't a direct action against God—we hurt Him, betray His trust, cause Him to be angry, and make Him sad.

And if your friends find out that you cheated? You could seriously damage your relationship with them, especially if there was money on the line. Cheating in golf while there was a bet on the game proves what you really value. When you cheat to win the bet, it proves that you valued your money or your pride more than you valued your friendships. If your friends find out that you cheated, they will justifiably feel like your wallet is more important to you than they are. That will cause permanent damage to your friendship with them. Would that be worth the cash?

As a golfer, you are responsible for your own integrity. Like I said earlier, there's no referee watching you in golf. You need to know that you have behaved honestly and lived up to the reputation that you want to have. Living with integrity means that our outward actions reflect the things that we believe and what we say we believe. So if we say that we are followers of Jesus, then we need to act like it! Cheating on a golf game is not a great way to prove that we are followers of Jesus.

The same thing is true in the rest of our lives, of course. We want to match our actions with our faith. Let me give you an example from the golf world again. Let's say you overhear someone in the locker room bragging about what a great golfer he is and how he has a really low handicap. You see him later showing off what he calls his "professional" clubs (whatever that means) to others. But when you see him on the course, he's playing an ugly round of army golf from one side of the fairway to the other. He tried to talk himself up as an amazing golfer, but he was no better than the average duffer. His foursome knows the truth, but he tried to make everyone else believe something different.

We can have the same problem in our Christian walk. We can learn to talk like a Christian, dress like a Christian, even do some of the activities that Christians do, while we are still happily and unrepentantly sinning every day. Our family probably knows what we're really like. Our friends might know. God definitely knows. But we might have strangers and casual acquaintances fooled. We are not living with integrity. 1 Samuel 16:7 says, "The Lord does not look at the things people look at. People look at the outward appearance, but the Lord looks at the heart." If this is how we are living, we need to find a way to make our outward appearances match up with our hearts. The best way to do that is to invite God in to clean our hearts up.

Golf can call us to be better people if we play with honesty and integrity. There's something about knowing that we did the right thing *even though* no human being was watching that is very encouraging. Like a child eager to please his father by doing well, we can rest in the knowledge that God saw our correct choice and that it pleases His heart.

GRATITUDE

Rejoice always, pray continually,

give thanks in all circumstances;

for this is God's will for you in Christ Jesus.

1 Thessalonians 5:16-18

WHAT ARE YOU THANKFUL FOR? Most of us can think of a few things off the top of our heads: our spouse, our children, our job, the warmth of the sun or the smell of the rain, and so on. When we stop to count our blessings, we can usually think of several. But if we're honest, I think we have to admit that most of us don't live in every moment counting our blessings. We leave the house late in the morning frustrated at our family. We like getting paid but we hate the guy we work for. The sun is too hot or it's raining too hard. You get the picture. Even though there are plenty of things to be grateful for, we all have moments when we stop living in gratitude and start to take the many good things in our lives for granted.

I remember this one fellow that I saw at my local course. He was loud and abrasive, swearing at the top of his voice every time he had a bad shot, throwing his used cigarette butts on the ground, and spitting on the grass.

He was even cheating! At first, of course, I was afraid of him and irritated with his behaviour. And then two things dawned on me about this guy. First of all, he obviously wasn't having a very good time. He had come out to the golf course to play a game of golf, but he clearly wasn't having fun doing it. Secondly, I thought, he must be taking the golf for granted. Really, being able to golf is a great privilege. It requires a lot of time and money, more than many people can afford. When I realized that this rude fellow was taking golf for granted it made me rethink how I felt about the game. I think since then I've been grateful for the opportunity to golf and it has made me more relaxed and patient as a result.

How much is enough? Can we ever find a place where we're just satisfied? Because we live in a world driven by consumerism, the answer to that question is "no, we will never be satisfied." There will always be more that we can buy to try to find happiness. But if we learn to live with gratitude for what we *do* have, it helps us to fight against the temptation to be unsatisfied with everything. I think we sometimes live our lives the way we play golf: always looking for the next best score. We want to shoot 100. Once we do that, are we satisfied? Having reached that goal, will we be happy? Probably not. Now we want to break 90, then 80, then be a scratch golfer. Are we satisfied? No, now we want to play a sub-par round.

Don't get me wrong: there's nothing bad about working hard to improve our golf score or our lives. But we need to live with gratitude while we do it. Even though it is good to improve, we should try to be thankful for each small step that we make, and for all the things that contributed to that success. When we adjust the posture of our hearts from grasping to gratitude, then we will find that there are endless reasons to be grateful. When we begin to live in gratitude, it changes how we look at everything. The grateful heart celebrates victories and challenges, because challenges are opportunities to grow. When we live in gratitude, we learn to be thankful for the process that gets us to our goal instead of just being thankful for the goal itself. We might find that we are even more grateful for the results of the process when we live that way. If the process is hard, then how much more grateful are we to have achieved a great result?

The grateful heart takes nothing for granted. Instead of believing that we are owed something, the grateful heart gives thanks for everything. If we get a lucky bounce that makes it easier to get a great score, we are grateful for that luck instead of treating it like something we expected to happen. If we get an unlucky bounce, then we bite our tongues before complaining about it, because we know that bad bounces are inevitable. I would encourage you to try to count your blessings every day, including the blessings that happen on the golf course. I think you will find that you enjoy yourself more and are more encouraged than you were before.

GRACE

---

*I became a servant of this gospel by the gift of God's grace
given me through the working of his power.*

Ephesians 3:7

---

*But he said to me, "My grace is sufficient for you,
for my power is made perfect in weakness." Therefore I will
boast all the more gladly about my weaknesses,
so that Christ's power may rest on me.*

2 Corinthians 12:9

---

*But by the grace of God I am what I am, and his grace to
me was not without effect. No, I worked harder than all of
them—yet not I, but the grace of God that was with me.*

1 Corinthians 15:10

H AS ANYONE EVER GIVEN YOU a present when you weren't expecting it? That's a pretty nice feeling, especially when the gift is something precious or meaningful. It makes you feel loved and valued by the gift-giver. It's even more powerful when you and the gift-giver haven't been getting along, or if you had done something to hurt that person. In fact, most human beings will never give you a special gift if you did something hurtful to them first.

That's what's so mind-boggling about grace. God gives us His grace even though we've already done terrible things to hurt Him. He gives it to us as a gift, with no strings attached. In fact, this gift of grace is so valuable that we could work for a thousand years in the highest paying job in the world and still never be able to afford to buy God's grace. What makes it so valuable? It's an all-access pass to eternal life—not just after we die, but starting right away! God's grace gives us the power to break free from our life of sin and start living an abundant life filled with His Spirit.

Throughout this book we talk about "lucky breaks" or having good or bad luck on the golf course. I don't believe luck is a power that we can earn or control in any way. I don't think there's a spirit or god we can please to make ourselves lucky. Luck is just random chance. It's statistics. But grace is something more powerful. God gives us grace when we don't deserve it. Grace is not something we can earn. Even the best people—say, like Mother Theresa—still need grace.

Think about it this way: how often do the touring professionals shoot a 59? It's pretty rare, isn't it? At the time I am writing this book, only six men and one woman have scored 59 in a professional tournament. These are the best golfers in the world, so you'd think they would be getting lower and lower scores all the time. But the barrier of 60 is obviously incredibly hard to break. All of them are or were top-of-the-leaderboard golfers, but there are dozens of golfers who have comparable records. It wasn't just hard work or sheer talent that earned them a 59. Some might argue that it was only luck, just statistics. But with only seven 59's over the course of thousands of tournaments, that makes for what the experts call a "statistical outlier." In other words, it's a bit freaky.

So, I would argue that shooting a 59 is a gift, like grace. It's not something that these golfers earned, nor is it something that they deserved. It was given to them for free. The only thing that makes it different from God's grace is that His grace is available to everyone, where those 59's are rare and only available to a very select few. The other word we might use to describe shooting a 59—or, say, making a hole-in-one—is that it is a miracle. Only God can make that happen. Even the best golfers in the world can't produce a hole-in-one whenever they want it. As Paul writes, "But by the grace of God I am what I am, and his grace to me was not without effect. No, I worked harder than all of them—yet not I, but the grace of God that was with me." (1 Corinthians 15:10) Paul starts to brag about all the hard work he has put in, but then he points out that he can only brag about the grace of God that did it all. Only God can make it happen.

Another golf-grace is the First Tee program. This program is available to kids from all walks of life and allows them to experience not only the game of golf, but also provides mentorship and instills in them the values of good sporting behaviour and good manners. This program is not-for-profit and therefore gives all of these things to these kids as a gift—not something they earned or even necessarily deserved, but something that is of great value in their lives. It's a grace.

Just like those kids who will now grow up with great potential and the gift of a life-long sport, those of us who have received God's grace can credit only Him with the life that we lead. God's grace empowers us to live our lives abundantly, to serve Him, and to be filled with His Holy Spirit. We don't even have the power to confess that Jesus is Lord without the grace of God! We don't deserve this grace any more than those kids were just born deserving the chance to learn how to golf. Frankly, we didn't deserve the chance to become golfers, either. Both grace and golf are gifts that we have been given. If that doesn't fill your heart with gratitude, I don't know what will.

Now, I don't want it to seem like we just take, take, take. If we get a present from someone and then just thank them for it but never unwrap it, what good is the gift? If we accept God's grace, but then never let it work in our lives, then it's as if we left the present on the shelf still in its paper and ribbons. Or if we want to think about it like golf, it's as if someone taught us to golf and gave us some clubs and then we never practiced. We might show up on the golf course and wonder why on earth we're playing so badly. We might blame the weather, or bad luck, or the course designer, but the real culprit is that we aren't practicing with the gifts we were given.

So it is with grace. If we accept grace but never use it, we're wasting it. Like Paul says in the quotes at the beginning of this chapter, grace gives us the power to serve God *and* it is sufficient—which is to say that it's all the power we will ever need to serve God. It really is a gift that keeps on giving. You don't need to worry about spending it all at once. There's always more, though as Paul warns, we need to be careful not to abuse God's grace by just continuing to sin (Romans 6:1-2). We will continue to sin, so we will need regular grace injections, but we shouldn't do it on purpose! Remember also that grace is a gift that's made for sharing with others, so feel free to give it away over and over again. For that matter, golf is the same: share it with everyone you know! Your love for the game will only grow when you do.

HUMILITY

Do nothing out of selfish ambition or vain conceit. Rather, in humility value others above yourselves, not looking to your own interests but each of you to the interests of the others.

Philippians 2:3-4

Live in harmony with one another.
Do not be proud, but be willing to associate with people of low position. Do not be conceited.

Romans 12:16

I THINK WE CAN ALL agree that our society values pride. Being proud of who you are and what you do is just normal for most people. That pride sometimes leads us to believe that we are most important person in the world and that we are extremely talented, even when that isn't the case. On the other hand, there are people who struggle to ever see themselves as good enough or having any talents. They think they're useless or broken. Are those people humble? Sadly, no. They are suffering from low self-esteem, but that's not the same thing as humility.

In my opinion, humility is the ability to see ourselves clearly as we really are: the way God sees us. That means we don't puff ourselves up with pride, thinking we're better or more important than we really are, and it also means that we don't put ourselves down, thinking we're losers or not important at all. As Paul tells the Philippians in the quote above, humility means valuing others more than ourselves and taking care of other people's interests before we take care of our own. Being humble is something that our society does not value. The world's view is that humility makes you a pushover and a doormat. God's view is that it makes you like Him.

Humble golf is Godly golf. It's also really difficult to achieve. We can be tempted to gloat about our victories and good shots, or to put ourselves down when we make mistakes or get unlucky. But if we want to play humbly, we need to acknowledge our real abilities. Our score will tell the truth about how well we play. We don't need to brag, building ourselves up as amazing players. If we don't have the strength to play from the tournament tee, that's okay. Play from the white tee or the red tee if that's what makes the game fun for you. There's no shame in it, and don't let anyone tell you otherwise. We also don't need to act like we aren't any good while quietly playing an under-100 round. Relax, have fun, and let the score you get speak for itself. Putting yourself down when your score tells another story is called false humility, and it is usually just another form of pride. And if you aren't a great golfer yet, you don't need to apologize for that, either. Everyone is a beginner at some point, and no one is born with a golf club in their hands.

Speaking of which, more experienced golfers need to remember that everyone was a beginner once. Playing humbly means putting other people's needs before our own. So, if you're playing with a beginner, then respect their ability level. Don't make them play the blue tee. Don't make them feel rushed if they're having trouble moving the ball long distances. Offer advice only if they ask for it, and always wait patiently for them to finish the hole. Golf is meant to be fun and it's meant to be shared, so don't let your ego ruin the game for a less-skilled player. Surrendering your pride won't hurt your game, and it will make the golf course a more welcoming place to newcomers and those who are struggling.

When we behave proudly, it's kind of insulting to the people in our lives. When we act like we're the best, we usually forget to give credit where credit is due. Even without mentioning God, that is like neglecting to mention all of the people who have helped us on our golf journey: the coaches we have had, a parent that drove us to the course in the early morning or simply helped pay for the green fees for our round, and anyone else who gave their support and encouragement. The humble golfer is quick to recognize the many people who have helped them become good at the game, because he or she is happy to put the interests of others before their own interests.

Proverbs says that pride goes before destruction (Proverbs 16:18). That means that when we get cocky, we are likely to start missing the mistakes we're making, and then suddenly we find ourselves flat on our faces. If you are really interested in getting better at playing golf, dump the pride in the parking lot. A humble spirit will make you a better student of golf, since you won't be defensive of your abilities and you won't think that you've already learned everything you need to know. Learning to golf well takes a lifetime! There's no shame in acknowledging that you have more to learn. I'm willing to bet that becoming a more humble golfer will help you to enjoy the game more. It certainly did that for me!

CRITIC

DO YOU KNOW WHO THE best golfers on TV are? Well, based on what I've seen when watching professional golf, it must be the commentators! They always seem to have a critique of the top golfers' swings and putts and strategies, so I guess they must know more than those pros and their instructors. Of course, I'm joking. I know that the commentators are very talented and experienced golfers. But even they would admit that it's easier to see mistakes and misses from the booth than it is on the fairway. In football there's the old joke about the "quarterback" who always has an opinion about how the game is played—from the comfort of his favourite living room chair. Golf fans can be the same, of course. It's easy to pick apart someone else's swing when you're sitting in your living room or in the stands around the green.

I've met people who try to play like they're touring pros, too. After watching lots of golf on TV, they try to play like the big names they see there: the men and women who make playing great golf look *so easy*. So these fans do things like trying to play from the black tees because they presume that they are as good as the pros. But usually that's not the case, and they often slow down play for everyone as they try to make up the distance. To be fair, I understand why they want to believe that they play better than they really do. Golf is truly difficult and it's a real blow to the ego when we have to accept our actual skill level. It's a lot easier to criticize the pros we see on TV (or other golfers at the course) than it is to criticize ourselves. As the old saying goes, the truth hurts. It's as though we have a telescope on ourselves and a microscope on everyone else, when really it should be the other way around.

I fear that sometimes we get this way as Christians, too. Especially when we've been Jesus-followers for a while, or grew up in the Church, we can start to get it into our heads that we are good enough to judge other people. I've really noticed this when it comes to listening to preachers—and I'll confess it's something that I've done, too! After you've heard enough sermons, there comes a temptation to start criticizing the preachers. You might think to yourself, "Pastor So-and-So preached about this passage so much better than this guy." Or maybe you silently tut-tut when the preacher stumbles in reading or loses his or her place.

It's bad enough to be judging the preacher, but the worst problem is that this moves us from active participation in Christianity to being armchair preachers. It's easy as pie to sit in the pew every Sunday and silently judge the delivery of the sermon. What's *hard* is actually getting out of the pew and *doing* the things that the preacher is preaching about! Anyone can "commentate" on a sermon or on other people's Christian walk. The hard thing is trying to do it yourself. And just like golfers who learn—painfully—that they aren't as good as the pros on TV, it can be a blow to the ego when we try to follow Jesus and find ourselves struggling all the time. We might think we're as mature in the faith as our pastor just because we're good friends with him or her, but that doesn't make it so. There's a reason they're the pastors and we're not!

It's easy to talk-the-talk as a Christian, especially when you've been in the Church for a while. There's a sort of Christian-ese (like legal-ese) that we pick up and we learn what to say and how to say it in order to *sound* holy. But we need to resist the temptation to just *sound* holy and actually try to *be* holy. Rather than criticizing others, we need to take action and do something with our faith. James says it well: "What good is it, my brothers and sisters, if someone claims to have faith but has no deeds? Can such faith save them?" (James 2:14) Our faith is our business and other people's faith is their business. We need to stop trying to be critics and instead we need to be active participants in our *own* walk with God. That's hard work, and it takes a lot of humility. God knows that some of us tee-off from the black tees and some of us from the white, and He's okay with that. He made us all with unique capabilities and strengths and He loves us all just the same. So if you've found yourself being an armchair Christian, don't be afraid to get up, swallow your pride, and try out the Christian walk. The only Commentator who matters is Jesus, and He's already your biggest fan.

100 Excuses

"Do not store up for yourselves treasures on earth,
where moths and vermin destroy, and where thieves break
in and steal. But store up for yourselves treasures in heaven,
where moths and vermin do not destroy, and where thieves
do not break in and steal. For where your treasure is,
there your heart will be also."

Matthew 6:19-21

HAVE YOU EVER NOTICED HOW some people seem to be really eager to get together with you, and then you find out it's because they need to borrow money? But then, when you need the money back, it's almost impossible to find time to meet up? Suddenly that person is terribly busy and they always have an excuse for why they can't make their appointment with you. Golfers have a similar problem. When someone's game is off, there can be an endless flow of excuses explaining why: "I have a lot on my mind," or "the weather is not cooperating," or "I'm tired," or "Things at work are stressful," and so on, and so on. The funny thing is that most people won't make the same excuses when they're playing well or when they make a great shot. No golfer, after making a thirty-foot putt, will say, "Oh, that was probably only because I had extra fruit with breakfast this morning."

Many of us find reasons to make excuses as Christians as well. I know a fellow who is almost always late for service. Each Sunday, our church service starts promptly at noon. This fellow can be counted on to hurry into the church between 12:05 and 12:10 each week. He's a friend of mine, so over the years I've asked him why he's so often late. There's always a reason: "My kids were slow this morning," "my car wouldn't start," "traffic was terrible," "just having one of those days!" But honestly, he was five to ten minutes late *every week.* He wasn't giving me reasons, he was just making excuses. There are people in my church who live much further away than he does but somehow manage to make it on time despite traffic, kids, or car troubles. Most of them are not only on time, but usually seated comfortably before the service begins. My friend had developed a habit of making excuses, and it's something that we are all at risk of doing as well. Before I sound like I'm throwing my friend under the bus, I have to admit that I've made plenty of excuses over the years. I served for one year as an usher, but then I got tired of coming to church extra early. After that year, whenever I was asked to serve again, I always found a reason—really, an excuse—not to do it.

It's also easier to make an excuse than to apologize, and it's much easier to make an excuse than it is to change our behaviour. Excuses are red flags about what we treasure. Jesus says, "where your treasure is, there your heart will be also." When we make excuses, we're really telling people what our "treasure" is. Perhaps we treasure our time—like my friend and I did, in different ways—or perhaps we treasure our pride, making excuses for why our golf game is bad because we'd rather not admit that we're struggling. Perhaps our treasure is money or fame, and we're afraid we'll lose it if we admit we did something wrong. We've probably all heard or seen someone try to make the excuse that they didn't know something they did was wrong. Especially on the golf course, if someone breaks one of the rules, they might claim that they simply didn't know about that rule. Even pros try to get away with this! It takes courage to admit that you did something wrong. Be brave! Although some people may lord it over you, others will respect you for taking responsibility and being humble and honest.

When we're talking about eternal life, of course, we need to be extra careful. There will be no chance to make excuses if we find ourselves in the hot place instead of in heaven! If there is any chance that we aren't sure what is right or wrong, then we need to ask someone who *does* know. Consult a pastor or a more mature Christian. Be humble enough to admit that you don't know or that you're confused about something in the Bible. It's better to swallow your pride now than it is to do the wrong thing and then try to rely on the excuse, "I didn't know!"And God will show you so much grace in return for you having the courage to confess you did something wrong.

QUITTING

For I am convinced that neither death nor life,
neither angels nor demons, neither the present nor
the future, nor any powers, neither height nor depth,
nor anything else in all creation, will be able to separate us
from the love of God that is in Christ Jesus our Lord.

Romans 8:38-39

OW TEMPTING IT IS TO quit when something gets too hard! Whether it is our beloved game of golf, our prayer life, or anything else that we think we've failed at, we've all been tempted to throw in the towel and give up at one time or another. But there's one thing that we can't quit: being loved by God. And that can make all the difference.

Have you ever seen someone "rage quit" a round of golf? Perhaps you've even done it yourself! A six-iron is thrown into a water hazard or a traitorous putter is broken over a stone, our clubs are sold on Craigslist and our shoes shoved into the back of the basement closet. "Never again! I quit!" we cry. We wonder why we've spent so much time and money only to play such a terrible round. We decide it isn't worth it. Eventually, though, the call of the fairway becomes too strong to resist and we buy new clubs, dig out the shoes, and head back to the course.

Obviously this is not the best way to deal with playing a bad round. When something goes wrong with our game, instead of quitting we should go back to the basics. We might take some lessons with the club pro or spend more time on the driving range. We'll review the tips in magazines and try to make adjustments to our swing. Instead of just practicing our favourite parts of the game, we'll brush up on the basics of every part so that we can find every place where we need to improve. We'll play the round one shot at a time, not thinking about the shot that we just made or planning for the next shot. We'll be in the moment. Most importantly, we recognize that bad rounds will happen. We aren't golf-playing machines and even the best of the pros won't lead every round. Instead of quitting, we need to be like a Bobo Doll, bouncing back up when we get knocked down.

The same thing can happen as we try to follow Jesus. We find ourselves sinning—again—doing the things that we swore we'd given up. Or else we get frustrated because we've been asking God for the same things in prayer over and over and still we haven't gotten what we've been asking for. So we stop doing our daily quiet time or we quit going to church. We put our Bibles away at the back of the bookshelf. "I quit!" we think. But hopefully, just as in golf, we eventually find ourselves lured back to church or unexpectedly praying to God.

When we pray, we need to remember that God knows what is best for us. We might become frustrated when God doesn't seem to be answering our prayers, but remember that sometimes when God answers our prayers, He has to say, "NO." Think of it this way: if a child asks his mother for a knife, she isn't going to give it to him even if he thinks he really, really needs it. She knows that the knife is dangerous for him and, because she loves him, she isn't going to give him something that will hurt him. We need to trust that God loves us and that *absolutely nothing* can take His love away from us. So even when He doesn't give us what we ask for, we need to trust that He knows what is good for us. Instead of quitting our faith, we just keep trying to follow Him.

Just as in golf, giving up on our faith is not the best way to deal with our sin or our frustration with God. If we are sinning, we can't give up on our faith! In 1 Timothy 4:8, Paul writes, "For physical training is of some value, but godliness has value for all things, holding promise for both the present life and the life to come." So, our bodily (or physical) training in golf is of some value—golf *is* good for us!—but our training as followers of Jesus is valuable in *every* way, not only today but forever.

When we're struggling with sin, we need to train ourselves to be better followers of Jesus the same way we train ourselves to play better golf. We need to go back to basics. Instead of just reading the parts of the Bible that we like, we should start at the beginning—in Genesis—and read the whole Bible so that we can understand the whole story of God and his relationship with us. When it really comes down to it, we can quit golf because it is just a sport, but we can't quit our faith because it is important to everything in our lives, now and forever. Instead of quitting, we need to be like a Bobo Doll, bouncing back up when we get knocked down.

Sometimes, things get really bad in our lives, though, and it can be hard to see how to go on. Like golf or like our faith, we might feel that there is nothing left for us in life and we might be tempted to give up. We might think that we've screwed up too much or that we've failed too often and that the only thing left to do is to give up on life itself. I've seen people who just stop trying. They let life happen to them instead of living it themselves. They think that even God must have given up on them, so they just coast, waiting for life to end. This is why Romans 8:38-39 is so important! Nothing will be able to separate us from the love of God in Christ Jesus our Lord: not our sins, not our screw-ups, and not our failures! God loves us no matter what, and if He won't give up on us, then why should we give up on ourselves? If we take that love and hold onto it, it becomes the fuel that can help us keep going. We might not have any strength left to keep going under our own steam, but the love of God can fuel us day and night without end.

Life can be very hard sometimes. There are so many things that we might struggle with, including our own sinfulness and the sinfulness of other people. Just like learning to follow Jesus, when life is hard we need to get back to Bible basics. We especially need to learn about how much God loves us and wants to give us the gift of life. Each one of us is precious to Him, and He wants all of us to keep trying. He doesn't expect us to be perfect because He knows that only He is perfect. So He gave us His Holy Spirit to be like the best-ever club pro, helping us every step of the way as we live our lives. He also gave us the Church: a whole group of other people trying to follow Him and making mistakes and learning to do better together. Instead of quitting or giving up on trying, we need to be like a Bobo Doll, bouncing back up when we get knocked down. We might not bounce back very far—not at first—but if we keep trying a little at a time, we'll stand up again eventually.

Sometimes it helps to get some perspective, as well. Remember what it was like to be a teenager with a crush on someone? For a while it's like your whole life revolves around that person and you can't think about anything else. Maybe you even pluck up the courage to ask that person out. But then they tell you that they don't want to go out with you. Since your entire life revolved around that person, it feels like your entire life has just ended. What will you do without them? Your heart is broken. Even adults can get obsessed with people, ideas, and dreams in this way. We set all our hopes on one thing and then if it doesn't work out, we're crushed.

I recommend that when this happens you take some time to go out at night and look at the stars. Think about the size of the universe, the distance between the stars, the number of possible other planets out there. Now think about the fact that God knows every single atom of every single star in the sky by name. Suddenly your broken heart or your crushed dream seems a lot smaller, doesn't it? That doesn't mean that it isn't important to you or to God, but hopefully thinking about it this way helps you to get some perspective, which will help you return to your problems with fresh eyes.

Another way to look at life or our faith or golf is to think about the plots of movies. The best stories in the movies are the ones about comebacks. We are most captivated by the stories about people who've hit rock bottom or found themselves in impossible situations only to come back and beat the odds. Our lives can be like movies and we are writing the story as we go along. The movie doesn't end when the hero hits rock bottom! It has to keep going so that we can see the hero get back up again. As any golf fan knows, wire-to-wire wins aren't that interesting to watch. The best tournaments to watch are those where someone comes from behind on Sunday to win. Just like in the movies, people love to see an underdog win. Think about the exciting story of David and Goliath in 1 Samuel 17. David was a young guy, too small to wear King Saul's armour, so in nothing but his shepherd's clothes and carrying a slingshot instead of a sword, he faced down a huge soldier. David should have been squashed, but with God on his side, he knocked the giant out with a small stone. Talk about a come-from-behind win!

If we find ourselves at rock bottom, then it isn't time to quit, it's time to try to make a comeback. We won't be able to do it on our own, but we can trust God to help us, because we can never sink so low that his love won't find us. We can't quit on Jesus because he won't quit on us! Even if we feel like we've "broken our clubs" and "quit the game," Jesus will help us to get back on the course. We may not be able to find anything inside ourselves to motivate us, so we have to lean on the love of God to motivate us. Life might not always be beautiful and we *will* make more mistakes and sin again, but that won't separate us from the love of God. Just like that Bobo Doll, we can straighten up again and keep on trying.

SIN

What shall we say, then? Shall we go on sinning
so that grace may increase? By no means! We are those
who have died to sin; how can we live in it any longer?

Romans 6:1-2

A WELL-EXECUTED GOLF SWING NEVER comes naturally. We use muscles and postures in golf that we simply don't need to use (or use in this particular way) in everyday life. So when we begin learning to golf, we have to learn to use these muscles that we wouldn't naturally use under normal circumstances. We have to unlearn the natural way we want to swing. Think about how unnatural correct posture is when you swing as you bend, tilt, and turn. You want to maintain the angle between your upper body and your lower body throughout the swing, all while keeping your head still and your feet planted. It really doesn't feel natural, which is why it takes so much practice to learn. But we know that if we stop doing all the important things to swing properly, then we'll lose control over the ball. We train our physical bodies and allow muscle memory to form so that we can stop thinking about how all those unnatural muscle movements work. We keep training our bodies because we know that our muscles will begin to lose their memory within 72 hours.

Learning to live a God-honouring life is even harder than learning to golf, especially if we try to do it all on our own. The "natural muscle movements" that our spirits want to make will always lead us into sin. In order to overcome those natural sin-muscles, we need to learn to follow God's leading in our life. We have to develop muscles and postures that we aren't used to using. We use the commandments in the Bible to learn which muscles we shouldn't be using—that is, to learn what is wrong and also what is right. There are plenty of things in the Bible that we wouldn't know were wrong unless we were told. We also can listen to our consciences. Most of us have a God-given signal built into our minds that tells us when we're doing something wrong. It works even more strongly when we've read the Bible to learn God's law, and it works the most strongly when we welcome the Holy Spirit into our lives to give us minute-by-minute coaching.

When we sin, it's like we're using our untrained swing. We have no control over our lives and where they are going because we're using our small muscles—in golf, we mean the hands and wrists instead of the big muscles like our torso and glutes. Sure, it may feel the most comfortable to use those every-day sin-muscles, but we also have to see we'll suffer the consequences. We'll probably end up shanking the ball way off into the rough. We have to build up the muscles and postures we aren't used to using, especially the big muscles that will give us the most control over our lives. We need to spend time daily in prayer because nothing helps us avoid sinning more than listening to the voice of God. We need to read the Scriptures that He gave us for our instruction. And we need to spend time every week worshipping in a community of others just like us, all learning to follow God together. Both our spiritual life and our golf game require discipline. Paul even equates the spiritual life to sports (1 Corinthians 9:23-27) and recommends disciplined training to keep our bodies in submission to our spirits.

Let's think about sin using a medical metaphor. Doctors tell us that every cell in our body has the potential of becoming cancerous. When the cell is working the way it should, everything is okay. But when the cell is provoked a certain way, it changes and grows into a cancer. We all have the potential for sin. Given the wrong circumstances, any of us can be provoked into sin. That's why we need to prevent that from happening by keeping our spirits healthy through the reading of Scripture, prayer, worship, and other Christian activities. Sometimes, like with cancer, there is nothing we can do to prevent sin. We are all born with sin ready to break out from inside of us. Thank God for His mercy and grace in those moments when we sin and need to repent again.

When we started learning to golf, it was awkward and uncomfortable using those big muscles and those strange postures. When we first start living a Christian life, things can feel awkward and uncomfortable as well. We have to bear with that awkwardness and know that it will get better. And we have to remember that whenever we need help, we can ask the Holy Spirit. He's our coach, ready to help us train those muscles anytime, day or night. That's great news!

BREATHE

---

*"I have told you these things, so that in me you may
have peace. In this world you will have trouble.
But take heart! I have overcome the world."*

John 16:33

YOU'RE READY TO TEE OFF at the eighteenth hole. It's around nine in the
morning—your foursome was the first out on the course. You've played
really well this round and coming off the seventeenth you're sitting at
82. If you could manage a birdie on this hole, it will be your best round ever.
Your friends know it, too. They're standing nearby, completely silent, watching as you address the ball. It's quiet, like even the birds and the wind itself are
holding their breath, waiting. Suddenly your hands grow damp and you feel
like your friends' eyes are burning holes into the back of your shirt. Your vision
blurs and the club feels like it weighs three times more than usual. There's so
much pressure! *There's no way I can do this*, you think. Then you remember
the words of the great golfer Sir Nicholas Faldo:

Breathe. Just breathe.

You close your eyes and take a few slow breaths in through your nose and out through your mouth. The world around you falls away and it's just you and the ball. You adjust your grip and confidently begin your backswing.

I don't know how the story ends, but I know what the moral is: keep breathing! It might sound obvious, since it's not like we can *stop* breathing, right? But when we're in high-pressure situations, we do sometimes start holding our breath or hyperventilating. Our bodies stop getting a steady, calm flow of oxygen and our panic grows. If we're playing golf, we might find that we lose our concentration and forget the things we know about posture and grip. We might start using our small muscles instead of our big ones and throw our swing off completely. Taking a few slow, deep breaths is a great way to calm ourselves down when we're feeling anxious and to help us re-centre so that we can concentrate and stay in the moment.

Although breathing can help us centre our minds at any time, there's something more we need to do to help ourselves get centred in our lives. We need to pray. I think we need to turn to prayer the way we turn to breathing—in fact, we can do them both at the same time! Prayer should be as natural to us as breathing in and breathing out, and it's just as vital to our spiritual health as breathing is to our physical health. Prayer is the spiritual form of breathing. When we're under pressure in our daily lives the way we can feel under pressure on the golf course, we could be tempted to "use our small muscles," which is to say, to sin. It's easy to revert to our sinful nature when the going gets tough. We might try to turn to our addictions—like drinking or gambling or shopping or overeating—to help us cope with the pressure. That's the same as using our small muscles instead of our bigger muscles in our golf swing. If we stop and pray instead I think we'll find ourselves getting back in control of our lives.

I am very encouraged by the verse at the beginning of this chapter. Jesus says, "In this world you will have trouble. But take heart!" When I read that,

I feel like He's saying, "Be bold!" When I take to heart that He is in charge and that He has overcome the troubles of this world, it's as strengthening as a breath of cool, clean air. When we feel overcome by the temptations and troubles of this world, it's like we remember Jesus saying, *Pray. Just pray.* In fact, in Matthew 6:9, He even tells us how to pray (it's the Lord's Prayer). When we pray to God and ask Him not to lead us into temptation, but to deliver us from evil, He will be faithful. And just like when we take a deep breath to calm ourselves, His Holy Spirit will be there to help us find our spiritual centre.

Without these deep breaths or calm prayer to help us, we run the risk of choking. Wouldn't it be sad if the story at the beginning of this chapter ended with you continuing to panic and then triple-bogeying the hole? We've all seen great golfers choke after playing really well throughout a tournament or round. Sometimes the pressure just becomes too much to bear and they can't seem to keep control over their game. It can happen to holy people, too. In 1 Kings 19, we read the story of Elijah, who was a great prophet of God, but still ran away like a little child and hid under a bush when he was threatened by the infamous Queen Jezebel. Instead of stopping to pray when she threatened him, Elijah lost faith. When he finally did pray, God took care of him. Even God's mighty prophets need a reminder sometimes to be bold!

Just like golf, our walk with God can sometimes feel lonely. It's true that we walk along with other people, just like we play in a foursome, but at the end of the day, we're responsible for our own decisions. No one can hit the ball for us, and no one can decide for us whether we're going to sin or to pray. Our friends can give us advice, but they can't breathe for us. Our Christian brothers and sisters can support us, but they can't save us. But in golf and in life we can walk along and talk with God. Take the time to pray. Take the time to breathe. Find your centre and you'll find your focus.

IDOL

Now if the foot should say, "Because I am not a hand,
I do not belong to the body," it would not for that reason
stop being part of the body. And if the ear should say,
"Because I am not an eye, I do not belong to the body,"
it would not for that reason stop being part of the body.
If the whole body were an eye, where would the sense of
hearing be? If the whole body were an ear, where would the
sense of smell be? But in fact God has placed the parts
in the body, every one of them, just as he wanted them to be.
If they were all one part, where would the body be?
As it is, there are many parts, but one body.

1 Corinthians 12:15-20

THE *POP IDOL* SERIES OF television programs has grown (at the time I'm writing this book) to cover over forty-five different regions in the world. I think the world loves these singing competitions because they give us all a hero to cheer on and support, tuning in to every episode to see what they'll do next. Watching golf tournaments on TV is less popular and the tournaments are far less glamorous, but I find that golf fans can be just as faithful to their golf idols. When you take a liking to a certain tour player, you want to watch all their tournaments, keep track of their career, and you'll probably remain faithful to them even through their slumps. You're a true fan, so you know they'll break out of that slump eventually, right? You might even try to play just like your favourite golfer. You might study their swing and read their golf tips and dress like them, then head out to the course to try to play the way they do. I mean, it works for them, doesn't it?

It can be fun to be a fan of a great golfer. There's nothing wrong with that. But I find that so many people idolize golfers that are nothing like them. I mean, Tiger Woods is 6'1" but I see guys much shorter than him trying out his swing (or at least, I used to see that). They might hurt themselves trying to swing like someone so much taller or stronger than they are. Even if they don't get hurt and even if they manage to make Tiger's swing work for them, there's not much of a chance that they'll start to play like Tiger Woods in his prime. They forget that it took Tiger a lifetime of golf training and thousands of hours of practice to become the great player that he is today. Instead of trying to copy Tiger or anyone else, golfers should concentrate on developing their own swing to be the best it can be. Like Arnold Palmer says in the 2013 Dick's Sporting Goods commercial: "Swing *your* swing."

I find the same thing to be true of Christians. We often have "Christian Idols"—great men and women like Billy Graham or Mother Teresa—and we want to be just like them. We read their biographies and the things they have written, listen to their sermons or speeches, and overall try to learn as much about them as we can. Then we might try to act the way that they do. But we forget that, just like a great golfer, it takes time and discipline to become a "great" Christian. If we want to be like Mother Teresa, we can't just suddenly move to India and live in the slums. That's all well-and-good if you feel that God is really calling you to do that, but don't expect to become a great holy woman overnight! Even Mother Teresa struggled with doubt and temptation and despair, I'm sure, and I know that it took her decades to establish her mission and work amongst the poor.

The same thing happens if we choose "Bible Idols" like, say, Joshua in the Old Testament or Paul in the New. You know what I love about the stories of people in the Bible? None of them are perfect except Jesus! All of them struggled with sin and doubt and despair, like any child of Adam and Eve. But even the ones who get things pretty close to right (like Joshua or Paul) still have areas that they need to improve. And they still took a lifetime to get to be the great leaders that we think about today.

My point is this: it's okay to have heroes. It's important to have other people that we look up to and strive to be like. But we need to remember that God made each one of us to be unique. We each have our *own* gifts and talents and the responsibility to build those up. Having a Golf Idol or a Bible Idol is fine, but you should try to become your own golfer or your own follower of Jesus. When you look for a hero, find someone with similar gifts and talents to yours if you're going to try to be like them. For example, I'm 5"6', so instead of trying to swing like Tiger, I watch the players on the LPGA tour, since they are closer to my height. There are lots of amazing people—golfers and Christians and Bible characters—that we can have as heroes. "But," Paul writes, "in fact God has placed the parts in the body, every one of them, just as he wanted them to be." (1 Corinthians 12:18) God made so many talented people to look up to, and I bet you're one of them, too! Be yourself and work to be like Jesus and you can't go far wrong.

POTTER & CLAY

Yet you, Lord, are our Father.
We are the clay, you are the potter;
we are all the work of your hand.

Isaiah 64:8

Does not the potter have the right to make
out of the same lump of clay some pottery for
special purposes and some for common use?

Romans 9:21

HOW DOES IT MAKE YOU feel to think that God is the one shaping your life as if you were a lump of clay? I don't think you're alone if you feel resistant to that idea. We live in a culture that encourages independence. We all want to be in control of our own lives and make our own destiny. So the idea that God might be taking a hand in our destiny can make us uncomfortable. I understand how that can feel. I think it's a pretty normal reaction. And I'm not saying that we should all sit around like lumps of clay waiting for God to work us over! We do need to act in order to serve Him. But we also need to accept his touch in our lives as He sends His Holy Spirit to show us where and when we need to change.

Who is the star of your life? Who is the leading actor? I think most of us would say, "Well, I am, of course!" It's only natural to believe that we are playing the lead role in the story of our own lives. The thing is, I've noticed that when I act like I'm the star of the show, then I'm more likely to do selfish and even sinful things. That's a part of what happened to me when I turned my back on what God wanted in my life, and I paid a high price for that! So I'm trying more and more to make God the leading actor in my life. I'm taking a supporting actor role. It's still really important, which is why awards shows have categories for supporting actors. But when God's the star, then He can shape what my life will look like. I let myself be the clay, and let Him be the potter.

Even in golf the best players don't play the leading role all of the time. Each week there's a new tournament and usually a new winner. The best players will still rise to the top of the leaderboard, but they will often trade wins as the season progresses. When I was thinking about this I was reminded of a bride and her bridesmaids. During the wedding, the bride is the centre of attention and her bridesmaids are there to support her. Usually at some time during the wedding reception, the bride will toss the bouquet and maybe one of her bridesmaids will catch it. Then, if the story holds true, that bridesmaid will be the next bride and will become the centre of attention for a day. The tournament leaderboards can be like that. The pack of the best players trade off the opportunity to be in first place. This isn't done on purpose, of course, but just because of the nature of the game. It's almost impossible to win week after week, and I've watched PGA seasons where the winner was different every week for over a month.

Because golfers can continue playing their sport for so many years, there's also the opportunity for their careers to go up and down like a rollercoaster. So for a few years they might be at the top of the tour rankings, but then they might slump for a couple of years only to make a comeback later. I see all of this as the work of the Potter's hand. He is shaping us and changing us, and, ultimately, He plays the true leading role. Even when we're winning, God is in charge and He might be preparing to shape us a little differently so that our circumstances change. We might not be the winner then, for a while. But we have to trust that He knows what is best for us. Sometimes He might want to use us for something special, and sometimes He might want to make us into something common. Both things are beautiful and important in His eyes. I find great comfort in that.

Iron Byron

He is the Rock, his works are perfect,
and all his ways are just.
A faithful God who does no wrong,
upright and just is he.

Deuteronomy 32:4

I N 1945, THE GREAT GOLFER Byron Nelson did something that's never been done since: he won 11 PGA tournaments in a row! That takes a lot of consistently great golfing. In 1963, engineers at the Battelle Memorial Institute invited Nelson to swing for them over and over again so that they could create a machine that used his perfect, consistent swing to test golf equipment to make sure that it is up to standards. They named the machine the Iron Byron after the great golfer that inspired its swing. The Iron Byron can make the same swing over and over again, all day long. That machine has the only perfect swing on the planet.

Most golfers will never be as consistent as Byron Nelson, and I think it's impossible to be as consistent as the Iron Byron. Human beings aren't machines, so we can't repeat the exact same motion over and over again.

For one thing, we'd probably get hurt. Our bodies just aren't built to repeat the same actions too many times. People who do that get repetitive strain injuries. So, we can't duplicate a swing, but we can try to copy it. What I mean is that we won't be able to make the exact same swing with the same force, rotation, speed, etc.—we can't duplicate a swing—but we can swing as closely as possible to what we did before—we can copy the swing. Do you see the difference? But the Iron Byron can duplicate a swing, because it is a machine.

There's only ever been one human being on earth who is able to obey the will of God perfectly, and that is Jesus. Because He is the Son of God, He is able to duplicate God's will, and do that consistently throughout His life on earth and in His eternal life in heaven now. We are normal human beings, descended from Adam, so we can only hope to copy the will of God. We are not God-pleasing machines, the way Jesus is. We can do our best to be consistent, but our sinful nature will interfere and we will eventually fail. We always want to be working towards being like Jesus, but we have to accept that in this life, we will never be perfect. Comparing our faith to Jesus' is like comparing our swing to the Iron Byron's. No matter how good a player might be—even Byron Nelson himself—they will never swing as perfectly as a machine.

Bobby Jones once said that golf is a game of misses. It's true, isn't it? We spend most of the round not quite hitting the ball where we want it to go, since we always want it to go straight into the hole! So, the fewer misses you make, the better your score. But you will miss. Life is the same. We will make mistakes. We want to be like Jesus, but because of our sinful nature, that's just not possible. His Holy Spirit will help us so that we make fewer mistakes, but on this side of eternity we will never be perfect. So, I try to aim to make fewer mistakes. If life is like the game of golf, then I'm always trying to lower my score. But since I can never play as consistently as the Iron Byron (that's Jesus, by the way), I will have to accept that there will be misses, and that that's okay, as long as I am trying to make fewer of them.

PROFESSIONAL VS. AMATEUR

Jesus called them together and said, "You know that those who are regarded as rulers of the Gentiles lord it over them, and their high officials exercise authority over them. Not so with you. Instead, whoever wants to become great among you must be your servant, and whoever wants to be first must be slave of all. For even the Son of Man did not come to be served, but to serve, and to give his life as a ransom for many."

Mark 10:42-45

RIGHT BEFORE JESUS CALLS THE disciples together in the verses above, two of them had been trying to convince Him to give them seats beside His throne. They wanted to be extra special when Jesus became King, though they didn't understand what that would take. These two disciples wanted to know who would be the most important in Jesus' kingdom. I think that's a part of human nature. We want to know who's in charge or who is the strongest or who is the best. That's why we have so many competitions and awards and golf tournaments! Even kids (and some adults) will argue about which superhero or super-monster is strongest (Batman vs. Superman or King Kong vs. Godzilla or Alien vs. Predator or Ali vs. Tyson or Nicklaus vs. Woods) or whose dad can beat up other dads.

Jesus says that being the first in the Kingdom of God means being a servant to everyone else. That feels really backwards to us, doesn't it? But that's what He did: becoming like a slave so that He could die and save us from our sins, and He's the Son of God (Philippians 2:6-11)! When Jesus calls people to be leaders in His Church, He wants them to be like servants to everyone else. We give special status to our leaders because of the sacrifice that they are making to serve us. We anoint them to be pastors, leading us in worship and teaching us the Word. They give up the chance to make more money in worldly jobs and to have more leisure time. It's hard work to be a pastor!

I see pastors as professional Christians. Like professional golfers, they dedicate their lives to doing one thing—pro golfers dedicate their lives to golf and pro Christians dedicate their lives to serving others. The rest of us are amateurs. We love to follow Jesus—just like amateur golfers love to play golf—but we don't have the special anointing that is given to pastors. The Church needs both professional and amateur Christians, though. We can't all be pastors!

Have you ever seen golfers who dress and act like they're professionals, but then shank the ball like any regular duffer? I think that we can be like that as Christians. We can act like we're as holy as the pastor—or holier, even— but really we're just amateurs. We have distractions that pastors don't have because our calling is to be in the world. Something that really bothers me is when I see older amateur Christians (say, like an elder or deacon in the church) who are trying to control a younger pastor. They seem to have forgotten that the pastor is the professional. The pastor has the special anointing and the special status that makes him or her a professional Christian...and also a servant. These folks think that because they are older, they are more holy, but

I don't think that's how things work in God's Kingdom. It's like these golfers I know who claim that they could beat an LPGA tour player in a round of golf just she is a woman. She might be a woman, but she is also a professional golfer! Because they are strong, these guys might be able to beat an amateur woman golfer, but not a pro who spends all her time working on her golf game.

We can't all be professional golfers or professional Christians. Pro golfers have special skill and pro Christians have a special anointing. In both golf and Christianity there is a place for amateurs. Anyone can play golf and anyone can follow God. All it takes is a love of the game or a love of God, since after all "amateur" means lover. In the Kingdom of God, the professionals aren't the best—they don't get to lord it over the rest of us like a superhero who wins a big match-up. So, be happy to be an amateur and leave the professional business to the pros. There's a place for all of us in the Kingdom.

RANGE FINDER

The horse is made ready for the day of battle,
but victory rests with the Lord.

Proverbs 21:31

I'VE SOMETIMES WONDERED IF WE could invent a robot golfer. There's a computer that can play championship chess, after all. We could give our robot the swing of the Iron Byron and fill its computer brain with all the information it needed about every golf course in the world. Maybe we could even give it range finder eyes so that it always knew how far it was from the green, the hazards, or the out-of-bound areas. Do you think that it would be a good golfer? I'm not so sure. I have a feeling that there are parts of playing good golf that require human intuition and gut feelings.

The range finder is a tool that was originally used by the military—specifically the artillery. It is a piece of technology that can measure the exact distance to a specific point. Some golfers use range finders as if having this technological tool will transform them into golf-winning robots. Sure, a range finder can be useful, especially if you are good at understanding how you need to swing to cover a specific distance. But despite its high price tag, a range finder only measures two things: distance and slope. It doesn't measure the humidity in the air, the air pressure, the wind speed and direction (especially important in the UK), or the temperature. All of these other variables can affect how your ball will fly.

I think some people use the range finder because it gives them the illusion of control. After what they spent on it, the darn thing should improve their game, right? But ultimately, their golf skill is the only thing that can make or break their game. The range finder is an expensive tool, but it's only a tool. It's very useful in the hands of a high calibre golfer, but it won't be as much use to a beginner and may even just slow down their play. I think that it's more important for a new player to develop a gut feeling for the game. I worry that when players depend too much on technology like the range finder, then they will lose their ability to play naturally. We should trust in our intuition and our body's ability to "feel out" the distance and angle and curvature of a shot. One thing a golfer should always remember is not to over-think!

We do the same thing in our lives that we do in our golf game. We try to find ways to take control. There are plenty of technological tools we can use to take control of our lives, especially as smartphones get smarter and smarter each year. We love to make plans and we want to keep our lives completely under control. We might even be tempted to drag God into our desire to control our lives. We pray to Him, asking for specific things that will make our plans come true. But God isn't a tool or a machine. He is a living Person, and He has a will of His own. He also has His own plans for our lives, and they might not be the same plans that we have made. We need to be flexible and follow the movement of the Holy Spirit, the same way that in our golf game we try to learn to follow our instincts and our gut feelings. Range finders and smartphones are great tools, if we use them the right way. But we don't *need* them. Trust your gut! Your body probably already knows how to hit that ball. And your spirit knows how to follow His Spirit as He leads you into an abundant life.

MULLIGAN

---

*Jesus replied, "Very truly I tell you, no one can see
the kingdom of God unless they are born again."*

John 3:3

---

*Therefore, if anyone is in Christ, the new creation
has come: The old has gone, the new is here!*

2 Corinthians 5:17

I MAGINE YOU'VE BEEN GIVEN THE chance to golf with Bill Clinton. No matter how you feel about his politics, playing golf with a former President of the United States is a pretty big deal! So, you're out on the course with Clinton. He's midway down the fairway and you and your friends are waiting nearby. He approaches the ball, looks up at the blue sky, down at the green open fairway, and blasts it into the only bit of water within sight. You don't know where to look! But he just laughs and says, "Gentlemen, I believe I'd like to take a mulligan on that one."

I think it would take a lot of guts to say, "No, Bill, I think you need to take a penalty on that shot." Unless you're George W. Bush, I don't think that's going to happen! Most people would join his laughter with a lot of relief and say, "No problem! Of course!"

Now imagine that you're on your way to play golf with your friends. As you were leaving the house, your four-year-old spilled juice all over your golf pants. You had to go and change. And then you got stuck in traffic. As you pull into the parking lot at the course, you can see your foursome is already at the first tee. You rush out to the course, dropping your bag onto the ground and hopping about trying to get your golf shoes on. Your three friends make their tee shots, carefully trying to ignore your antics. You hastily pull on your glove and approach the tee. You make your shot, but instead of sailing up into the air, it scuds along the ground to stop maybe twenty yards away. How embarrassing! You were so rushed that you made a complete mess of your shot.

"Hey, guys," you say sheepishly, "any chance you'd give me a mulligan on that one?"

Hopefully you have nice friends who would give you the chance to do the shot over. That's what a mulligan is, in case you've never heard of it—the chance to make a second shot without a penalty. Mulligans aren't allowed in competitive golf, so you won't see that happening in a tournament. But between friends during a regular, just-for-fun game, mulligans are allowed. And let's be honest: whether you're the President or just some guy, we all need a mulligan every now and again. That's true in our life as well, isn't it? We all need a second chance (or a third chance or a tenth chance) sometimes. Whether we're giving someone a bit of grace on the golf course or a bit of grace in their lives, it's always a good and precious gift.

When I think about what Jesus did for us, I think it's a holy mulligan. We were all headed to hell because human beings just can't stop themselves from sinning. God is so holy that it's against His nature to be in contact with something as sinful as human beings. But then God did something amazing: He gave the human race a mighty mulligan by sending His Son to pay the price for our sins. Jesus took the penalty for our bad shot. Because of Him, we get to keep playing, and even to live forever with our Holy God. How amazing is that? When we are born again in Jesus, we get our second chance at life, penalty-free. It's like Jesus ripped up our bad scorecard and gave us a fresh, new one.

If Jesus can do that for us, then I think we can all manage to give our buddies a break on the golf course when they need it, don't you? Grace and mulligans are contagious. Pass it on!

White House

---

*But the Lord said to Samuel, "Do not consider his
appearance or his height, for I have rejected him.
The Lord does not look at the things people look at.
People look at the outward appearance,
but the Lord looks at the heart."*

1 Samuel 16:7

---

*The fear of the Lord is the beginning of wisdom,
and knowledge of the Holy One is understanding.*

Proverbs 9:10

H AVE YOU EVER BEEN TO a golf course with a dress code? Most of them have rules about what you can wear on the course—no jeans, no shirts without collars, shorts and skirts no shorter than four inches, and so on. If you try to wear anything else, you will be turned away. There are other rules in place for the golf course, too, such as coming on time for your tee time. If you want to respect the other golfers, you follow the rules and the dress code.

Now, imagine you have the privilege of being invited to dinner at the White House. I bet that there are dress codes for that as well, but I'm sure that they don't need to be enforced. Who's going to wear jeans and a stained t-shirt to have dinner with the leader of the free world? I know if I was invited to the White House, I'd want to wear a really nice suit—maybe even a tuxedo—and buy my wife an appropriate new dress, and we'd probably show up at least two hours before dinner was supposed to start. I wouldn't want to disappoint the President by being late or wearing clothes that were disrespectful to the Office.

If we are willing to dress up for the President, or follow the rules at a golf course, then how much more should we be willing to dress up for God when we go to His house (that's the church, by the way)! Most churches nowadays don't have dress codes, though I think that each church has unwritten ideas about what is and is not appropriate clothing for church. But I feel like I should wear clothes that are suitable for visiting our God. I know that He looks more at my heart than at my outward appearance, but I want Him to know that I am making an effort when I come to worship. We shouldn't dress up for church to impress other people—church isn't the place for a fashion show—but if we would make the effort to dress up to respect the President, who is only a human being, then how much more should we make the effort for the Creator of the Universe!

So I try to dress and act respectfully at church. I don't always succeed, but I try. I aim to be there early or on time, and to dress well, but not over-the-top. I've also tried to teach my children how to dress and act at church. It's easy to try to impress people we can see, like the other golfers at the course or the President (if we should be so lucky). It's harder to remember to dress to impress our God, since we can't see Him. So next time you're getting ready to go to church, consider Who you're going to be visiting. It might make a difference in how you dress and act.

SABBATH

Then he said to them, "The Sabbath was made
for man, not man for the Sabbath.

Mark 2:27

L ET'S BE HONEST: IF YOU love golf and you love God, there's probably a
major conflict that goes on in your heart every weekend. Do I play golf
on Sunday morning, or do I go to church? It's certainly something I've
struggled with over the years. I'm sure it's something that Christian tour players struggle with. For an ordinary person, it's probably only possible to play
golf on the weekends, and there are so many things already competing for
your time, like family, chores, shopping, and so on. It can be very tempting to
skip church so that we can squeeze golf into our already busy schedules.

I'm not sure what the right answer is when it comes to honouring
the Sabbath. I know I've sometimes felt like Sabbath-keeping was a holy
obligation—I feel the pressure of the Holy Spirit on my conscience that it is
something that I need to do to stay right with God. I've also been really inspired
by stories of Christians who were faithful to keeping the Sabbath, especially
the story of Eric Liddell as told in the movie *Chariots of Fire*. Liddell was a

Christian and an Olympic runner from Scotland who refused to run the heat for the 100-metre event—his speciality—because it was on a Sunday. He was under a lot of pressure from his countrymen, including the Prince of Wales! But he stuck to his beliefs and inspired people around the world. I certainly have found his story inspiring, and also a little convicting. I don't know if I have the same strength that he had to hold true to his beliefs.

I do wonder, though, if there's a connection between times when I've been missing Sunday services regularly and times when I've been struggling in my life. I'm not sure, but it's something that comes to mind for me. I think that the question we need to ask ourselves is, "Am I bothered about missing church?" If we never think twice about skipping church to go golfing, then I think that's a bad sign. We should at least struggle with the decision! But as I've said, I don't have the answer. I think each one of us needs to examine our hearts and decide where our priorities are. Are we putting our own convenience and pleasure above our duty and desire to worship God? I think that's the real question about how we spend Sunday mornings. The answer to that question has to be worked out between you and the Holy Spirit.

Not for Sale

Then Peter and John placed their hands on them,
and they received the Holy Spirit.

When Simon saw that the Spirit was given at the laying on
of the apostles' hands, he offered them money and said,
"Give me also this ability so that everyone on whom I lay
my hands may receive the Holy Spirit."

Peter answered: "May your money perish with you,
because you thought you could buy the gift of God with
money! You have no part or share in this ministry,
because your heart is not right before God.

Acts 8:17-21

Isn't money great? I mean, you can buy anything you need if you have enough money, right? Well, maybe not everything. Like The Beatles sang, money can't buy you love. I think many golfers have looked at their expensive clubs and the bills for their lessons and realized that money couldn't buy them a good golf swing. Many parents have wrung their hands and squeezed their wallets to send their kids to university only to discover that the young ones didn't have what it takes—all that money couldn't buy them smarts! And the most precious thing of all—the salvation of our souls—was too expensive for any of us to afford, so the Son of God paid for it in His blood. That's great news! It means that you don't need to be wealthy or smart or powerful to be saved, since Jesus paid it all.

Maybe money isn't that great after all. It can't buy me love, or a golf swing, or a good grade, or salvation. As Simon the magician learned in Acts 8, money can't buy the gifts of God, either. God's gifts come from Him free. They aren't for sale. But don't we all want to try the easy, quick way to get things, just like Simon the magician? Developing a good golf swing is hard work, so it would be so much easier if we could just go to the club pro and ask him to sell us a good swing. Becoming a better follower of Jesus would be so much easier if our pastor could sell us our sanctification. But those things are not for sale.

A good golf swing comes through practice and perseverance. We need to work hard if we want to develop the skill we need to be a great golfer. Following Jesus is the same: we need to work at our sanctification. No one can do it for us, and don't trust any pastor that tries to sell you some band-aid solution from the pulpit. If it sounds too good to be true, it probably is too good to be true! There are no magic words or instant answers when it comes to following God. All we need is a willing heart and a teachable spirit. God will show up if we are faithful and He will help us. But we need to be ready to work hard, the same way we do on the golf course and practice range.

Technology

Jesus answered, "I am the way and the truth and the life.
No one comes to the Father except through me."

John 14:6

I T SEEMS LIKE EVERY DAY there is a new club or a new ball or even a new pair of shoes available that will make our golf game better. Engineers are always finding different materials to use in our equipment and new ways of putting those materials together. Over the past one hundred years golf clubs have become lighter, more flexible, and have larger faces. Frankly, it's a lot harder to be a bad golfer now than it was in my grandfather's day. Although there are a lot of advantages to these newer club and ball designs, there are also some drawbacks. I think that the newer equipment sometimes makes us lazy about fixing the problems in our swing. Instead of practicing more and trying to iron out the faults in our swing, we just buy a different club that makes it easier to keep swinging the way we do now.

Let's be honest: there is a lot of ego in golf, so it makes sense that we want to hit the ball longer and with more accuracy. But really there are no short cuts to playing the game well. Technology may change, but the fundamentals of the golf swing haven't changed. Ultimately, buying new equipment isn't actually going to make us a much better player. We need to practice regularly and learn from our mistakes so that we can improve. The best players rely on technique more than technology.

Jack Nicklaus has argued, in fact, that we should stop making equipment that takes the challenge out of the game. His argument is that it is becoming harder to tell the difference between average players and good players *not* because there are more good players, but because the technology is hiding the average skill of the average players. He's also noted that because newer technology makes it easier to hit the ball a long way, course designers are forced to make longer courses. Think about it: with the right driver, a modestly talented amateur golfer may have a 250 yard drive. With so many players using this technology, it's easier than ever to fly further and straighter, so designers have to compensate. Longer courses take up more land and require more water to keep them green. That takes a toll on our environment and it costs more to operate. I think that if we restricted the development of golf technology, we would see courses designed so that they were realistically challenging and where true ball strike ability and creativity would be rewarded.

In my mind, the way that new technologies have made us lazy in our golf practice is the same way that cultural changes sometimes make us lazy in our Christian practice. In our culture, ideas are changing all the time. That can be good and can provide us with new tools for following Jesus, but it can also tempt us to want to change things that shouldn't be changed. The truth in the Bible never changes, just as the fundamentals of a good swing never change. We can use new technologies or new ideas in our faith, but we need to be careful to hold to the truth in the Bible. In our lives, we might find that new ideas give us opportunities to sin just the way that a new club technology compensates for the faults in our swing.

As Christians, we always have to be careful not to take God's grace for granted, thinking that because God loves us, He will let us go on sinning (see Romans 6:1 and following). We have to learn the difference between what is legal and what is righteous. What I mean is this: there are things in our world that are legal, but they still aren't things that are good for Christians to do. Adultery is not against the law, but it is forbidden by God to break our marriage vows. Don't let cultural standards be like oversized clubs that make it easy to hit the ball. Learn to walk in God's way through practice, prayer, and Bible study and that will take you much further than the new ideas and passing cultural trends (Romans 12:2).

BRAND NAME

*But the Lord said to Samuel, "Do not consider his
appearance or his height, for I have rejected him. The Lord
does not look at the things people look at. People look at the
outward appearance, but the Lord looks at the heart."*

1 Samuel 16:7

T HE OTHER DAY I HAD a difficult decision to make at the pharmacy. I had
come in with a prescription from my doctor and presented it to the
pharmacist. He disappeared behind the counter for a few minutes and
then reappeared with a printout from his computer.

"Here's the thing," he said, "I can dispense this medication to you, but
you'll have to pay for part of it out of pocket. If you want, though, I can give you
the generic version and your insurance will cover the full price."

At first I wasn't sure what to do. My doctor, I supposed, had chosen that
brand of medication for a reason. What if the generic version didn't have the
right ingredients? What if wasn't going to be as effective as the brand name
medication? I didn't really want to pay any more for the prescription than I
needed to, but I didn't know if I could trust the generic brand to get the job

done as effectively as the brand name.

I think sometimes golfers face the same decision when it comes to the courses they play on. Some people will seek out the most famous (often also the more expensive) courses in an area and only play on those. It's as if the "brand name" course will make them a better player than they actually are. But does playing on a famous course make them play any better than a golfer that has shot a 77 at a good "generic" public golf course? Is there a difference in their ability because one golfer is playing at a well known or even famous golf course and the other player is playing at one that is neither famous nor expensive? Of course not!

Even if a golfer is using a set of brand name clubs and he's playing against a buddy who is equally matched in skill, determination, and ambition, but who is using a set of no-name clubs, it does not guarantee that one will play better than the other. The clubs really do not make all that much difference for amateurs. They are both designed to achieve the same result: to hit the ball accurately toward the hole. If you have a good swing and practice the game, then you will be able to play well with almost any set of clubs. I know that can be hard to accept. Frankly, we live in a culture that is always trying to sell us the next-best-thing, and brand names are used to do that. It takes some work to believe that brand names don't matter as much as we're told they do.

I hate to say it, but I think the same thing is true at church as well. Let's say there are two people trying their absolute best to follow Jesus. One goes to the church nearest home and the other goes to a very well-known church. It is attended by some of the most recognizable people in town and has a big and beautiful building. There are famous preachers and popular worship leaders coming in on a regular basis. The church advertises its services on television. Clearly, this church is where it's at! But we have to wonder if the person attending it is really any more holy or righteous than the person at the "generic" church? Are their prayers to God really heard differently? Does God give priority to one over the other? Or is God simply looking at what is in each of their hearts? Just because one person goes to a big church doesn't necessarily mean that they have a big faith, and the small church member doesn't necessarily have a small faith.

Whether we're talking golf or faith or anything else, we need to learn that brand names can sometimes be an illusion. Sure, they offer familiarity but they don't guarantee quality. What I've learned is that very often what we bring to our golf game or our faith is more important than the name on our clubs or our church building. You're reading my book, so I know you're a pretty smart person. I know that you are smart enough to see past the advertising and the flashy lights to decide if something is really worth your money and time. A great golf game can happen on any course and with almost any clubs if you've put in the effort to practice beforehand. Following Jesus is possible anywhere in the world if we humble our hearts and trust in Him. He doesn't ask for brand names, and we don't need to, either.

Handicap

N O ONE IS A BORN golfer. Sure, some have a ridiculous amount of natural talent and can do things with a club that the rest of us could only imagine, but we all have to work at the game to improve. For the most part, we all start with a 30 handicap (which means hitting 30 shots over par for the course). We're all aiming to play the lowest score possible, right? In order to improve our handicap, we need to practice and play a lot. Realistically, though, we also have to accept that we can't lower our handicap forever. We don't want to get too comfortable or, like it says in the verse above, we might fall! Our handicap is never written in stone. The average male golfer has a handicap of around 16, and most women will find their handicap is around 28. Even if we do better than that, as we get older our handicap will go back up again. Even the legendary Arnold Palmer is not shooting what he was in his 20's. He's elderly now and shooting a very respectable game of golf for his age, but it is a far higher score at the end of the round than it was when he was a young man in his prime.

I think we find the same thing is true in our walk with Christ. Matthew 20:16 reminds us, "the last will be first, and the first will be last." I've found that there are people who've been going to church for over thirty years who have found their faith starting to fade. Sometimes they just know too much— about life or about the Bible. On the other hand, some folks that have just begun going to church are freshly feeling the Holy Spirit and find it easier to live joyfully and in the spirit of God's teaching. Just because someone has been at a church for decades doesn't necessarily mean they have a greater faith or spiritual life. We have to be careful not to automatically consider age or experience to be a sign of deep faith. That's not to say that an older, more experienced Christian won't have a strong walk with God still, just as it's possible for an older, more experienced golfer to play a great round of golf.

We say in golf that there's a price for a birdie. Scoring a birdie puts you on top of the world! But then your friends might say, "Careful, or you'll pay the birdie price!" Like that verse above says, "if you think you are standing firm, be careful that you don't fall!" In other words, after you birdie a hole you may ruin the next hole because you're too excited and think that you're going to have a great score for the whole round. Proverbs 16:18 famously says, "Pride goes before destruction, a haughty spirit before a fall." After a birdie, it is very easy for us to feel great pride, like we own the golf course. But if we aren't careful, the very next hole might be the worst of all. A low handicap golfer doesn't dwell on past achievements. They live in the present because they know that each hole is its own battle. They may have birdied the last hole but they put that thought aside and concentrate on the shot they're playing now. It's one shot at a time: staying in the present.

I want to emphasize how important it is to stay in the present. It might help you to think about how we give presents to one another. The present moment is a present that we get from God. We should be thankful for it! We are given each moment by God and we will learn to live abundantly if we can receive those moments as presents. Our handicap is a part of that present moment—don't dwell on the past moments or dream about the future ones. Accept the present moment exactly as it is, be grateful for it, and celebrate it (just like you would celebrate getting a present).

People with a low faith handicap are the same as golfer who maintain a low handicap. They don't think about their past "achievements" as a follower of Jesus; instead, they stay awake to what the Spirit is doing in their lives in the present. I think we always need to be asking ourselves, "What's my faith handicap today?" We can't stay fixed in the past. Good or bad, our "score" yesterday is gone and today is a new day. We won't gain anything by bragging about the past or feeling smug because we used to be really great Christians. We have to be accountable to today. How can we serve God in this moment?

Not to scare you, but a handicap is kind of like a ghost or a cockroach: you can't seem to kill it, and it's likely to creep out when you least expect it! Sometimes we'll be on a very easy hole, but we'll still shoot a high score because we have a specific handicap. If I shoot a 38 on the front nine, I still might shoot a 45 on the back nine. That handicap jumped up to say, "Boo!" I can't ignore it, but I can and must learn to live with it. I will continue to try to lower my score, but I will also recognize that God made me the way I am and be thankful for the gifts that I do have.

2 Corinthians 12:9-10 states, "My grace is sufficient for you, for my power is made perfect in weakness." It is common for many of us to complain about our handicap. But if we acknowledge our weakness, then we can see how God's grace is working in us. Each of us is given different skills and talents by the grace of God, and that is sufficient for us. Not everyone can be a tour player. What graces I have received I should be thankful for and accept that

it is enough. Sure, through practice we can improve in some ways but there will always be a handicap on what we are able to achieve. Be honest about your abilities in all things, not puffing yourself up or talking yourself down, and accept who you are. God made each of us unique and He loves all of us the same, whether we're scratch golfers or regular duffers. What is your faith handicap these days?

PLAYERS AND TOURS

But to each one of us grace has been
given as Christ apportioned it.

Ephesians 4:7

WHEN I READ THAT VERSE, it reminds me that each one of us is made to be unique and special in God's eyes. That doesn't mean that we're all going to be grand-slammers and shoot 59 and be famous. Being special to God doesn't mean that we'll be noticed by the whole world or even be very talented according to worldly standards. Some people have more talent and others less; some people are destined to be famous, and the vast majority of the rest of us are not. That's okay. Each of us is given our own set of talents to nurture and cultivate. In golf, you find the whole range of skill sets from the guy who only plays once or twice a year and is happy to get the ball on the fairway at least once a round, through the people who make a living teaching golf as club pros, to the stars of the professional tours. We all can enjoy the talents of the really gifted. That's the wonderful thing about watching professional tournaments on television! I enjoy watching the big professional tours and the talented individuals that play on them. For example, there's the Professional Golf Association (PGA) Tour, the Ladies Professional Golf Association (LPGA) Tour, and the Champions Tour, just to name the prominent North American tours. There have been some great golfers over the last century and I would like to tell you about some of the players I admire and the Tours that host them.

I want to begin by praising the LPGA's Founders Cup tournament. I think that it's so wonderful that they have a tournament that honours the legacy of the founders of the LPGA Tour. It's so important to remember our roots and to honour those who have gone before us, and I think that the LPGA does a superb job of that in the Founders Cup. This tournament holds the greatest significance in my mind by honouring the origins of the LPGA Tour.

I also want to give special attention to the Champions Tour. The players on this tour are all over fifty years of age. I've noticed that there is more maturity and richer, stronger camaraderie amongst the players of the Champions Tour than amongst their younger, perhaps more competitive colleagues on the PGA Tour. I have great respect for these men. I view them as warriors who are still fighting the good fight. Like General Douglas MacArthur told Congress, "Old soldiers never die, they just fade away." I think that by continuing their competitive golf careers on the Champions Tour, these players are proving that to be true of golfers as well as soldiers. As it says in Proverbs 16:31, "Gray hair is a crown of splendor; it is attained in the way of righteousness."

Golf has an amazing history filled with great players. One of the earliest great players on record was the great Scottish golfer known as Old Tom Morris, who died in 1908. He served the Royal and Ancient (St. Andrews Golf Course) as greenskeeper, club maker, ball maker, golf instructor, and course designer as well as being a professional golfer! In fact, Morris won the 1862 Open Championship by fifteen strokes over Willie Park. He held the record for the largest margin of victory in a major championship until Tiger Woods won the 2000 US Open by 15 strokes.

Next I'd like to tell you about Bobby Jones. You might know him as the father of the Augusta National Golf Course, home of the Masters Tournament. Jones was a graduate of Harvard Law School and played his entire career as an amateur instead of a professional. That means that when he played in a tournament and won, he couldn't take the money that was offered as a prize. He was playing for the glory only. I heard that one player claimed that Jones would never beat him because he played for money and Jones didn't, as if the money was the only thing that would drive a golfer to greatness. But that guy didn't realize that for some people, like Jones, the love of the game is every-thing. That's what *amateur* means, after all: lover. For Jones, that love of golf led him to win all the available major tournaments of his day as well as both the British and US Amateur tournaments. From Bobby Jones I learned that money isn't everything and that true love of the game is the key to greatness.

I've also really appreciated the golf game of Ben Hogan. A true Texas gentleman, Hogan was a grand-slam winner and even managed to survive a car accident, recover, and go on to continue being a winning golfer. Most committed golfers will be familiar with him through his book *Five Lessons: The Modern Fundamentals of Golf.* I owe so much of my golf game to that book! Have you noticed how many great golfers come from Texas? I can think of Ben Hogan, Byron Nelson, Tom Kite, Ben Crenshaw, and 2015's fast-rising star, Jordan Spieth, just to name a few. I don't know what they serve in the clubhouses down there, but I think I need some!

Next up is Arnold Palmer. I think we can agree that this is the guy who raised the profile of golf as a spectator sport as well as a sport you play. You can tell when you watch him play that he really loves the game. He strikes me as someone who is humble and generous. In fact, his fans call themselves

"Arnie's Army" because they are so devoted to him. His talent and his popularity earned him the nickname "The King." The way I see it, there are two kinds of kings: tyrants and kings who model themselves on Jesus. I think Arnie is more like Jesus than like a tyrant. He has such a humble spirit and doesn't think that just because he's talented, he's better than everyone else. I think that's why he has such devoted fans and why he's probably still the most influential figure in golf.

The next golfer I really admire is Jack Nicklaus. I'd say almost everyone has heard of him and knows that he's a great golfer. At the time that I'm writing this book, Nicklaus is the record-holder for the most major tournament wins. The thing I like about him is that he's obviously also a good man. In 2014, he received the Congressional Medal of Honor "in recognition of his service to the Nation [of the United States of America] in promoting excellence, good sportsmanship, and philanthropy." When I see pictures of him with his family, I can see that he has been so blessed with many happy children and grandchildren. His golf career didn't take over his life. He made space for his family and for doing good works. That's something I really admire!

Jack Nicklaus had a healthy rivalry with Arnold Palmer. Nicklaus appeared on the scene and challenged The King's supremacy on the tour. I think that Nicklaus knew that Palmer was better loved by the crowds, but I also think that Palmer knew that Nicklaus was the more disciplined golfer. Nicklaus was a perfectionist and I think that that was what made it possible for him to be such a successful, record-breaking player.

The last of the big three names in golf is Gary Player. He's been called the International Ambassador of Golf since his golf career has logged more travel miles around the world than any other athlete from any other sport! He hails from South Africa and has raised the popularity of the game there, as well as proving that great golfers don't just have to come from the US or the UK. In fact, Player is the only grand-slammer who wasn't an American! In 1965 he won the US Open, completing his grand slam. He was also known as the Black Knight (now the name of his own golf equipment company) because he chose to dress all in black, honouring the fact that he grew up in South Africa. His third nickname is Mr. Fitness because he demonstrates and advocates for true athleticism and healthy eating. His golf career continued comfortably into his senior years because he continued to keep in excellent shape. That's something to look up to in my opinion.

Finally we come to Tiger Woods. Tiger is definitely one of the most popular golfers of all time. He is certainly one of the most dominant players and there was a time when he was expected to break all the records, but at the time of this writing he hasn't beaten the records of Jack Nicklaus (18 majors) or Sam Snead (most wins), nor is he a member of the 59 Club. As he rose to greatness in the game, he was compared by Brandel Chamblee to William Wallace—the great Scottish freedom fighter—when he played his irons. His excitement over a great shot is contagious, and his signature fist pump is inspiring. I've no doubt that many young people have become golfers just because of Tiger Woods.

Sadly, unlike the other men I've described, Tiger's career has been overshadowed by his infidelity to his wife. As far as I can tell, his career began to go downhill at the same time. How disappointing that was for so many fans! It makes me question why there was no "Nathan" for Tiger Woods. Do you remember the story of King David and his affair with Bathsheba? You can read 2 Samuel 11 if you don't know it (see the end of this book). In 2 Samuel 12, one of the prophets of God tells King David a parable that shows the King how bad his sin really was. David repents and renews his covenant with God. In my opinion, there clearly was no Nathan in Tiger's life. Instead he was surrounded by an entourage of people who were getting rich and popular from his success. If they knew he was doing wrong, they didn't want to tell him because then they might be forced to get off the Tiger Train. I think that makes them partly responsible for Tiger's sin. Proverbs 16:18 says that pride goes before destruction. I think that it's possible that if his infidelity had never been disclosed, then Tiger might have gone on winning, with the appearance of his pride intact before the world's eyes. When his sin was revealed to everyone, his pride and the effects of his pride became evident and it seems to have had a devastating effect.

Many people believe—and maybe even Tiger himself—that he needs a change in his swing if he wants to start winning again. But there were still faults in his swing *while* he was winning. So, I'm not sure that what he needs is a swing change. I think he needs a change of heart. Quite honestly, I think that Tiger Woods needs to repent of his way of life and the things that he has done wrong. When I see him on television today, I see sadness in his eyes. I think he's trapped in regret. He reminds me of the rich young man who asked Jesus how to inherit eternal life and then went away sad when he heard the answer (Matthew 10:17-31).

In 2 Corinthians 12:9, Paul writes, "But [Jesus] said to me, 'My grace is sufficient for you, for my power is made perfect in weakness.' Therefore I will boast all the more gladly about my weaknesses, so that Christ's power may rest on me." When I was in high school, I was taught about Darwin's theory of natural selection—that only the fittest specimens of each species survive. I found that rather shocking. Now, as I have come to learn more about Jesus and His ways, I can't help but see the problems with the theory of natural selection. Jesus says that His power is made perfect in weakness, not in strength. I think that Tiger has been living and playing according to natural selection, but I think that if he turned his life over to God, then Jesus would show him that true power is made perfect in weakness, not in strength.

As I'm writing this book, Tiger has lost six years of his career to this disappointment. I really believe that if he had not been caught in his infidelity, then he probably would have gone on shattering records. But I think that it was God's plan to introduce hardship into Tiger's life—not to punish him for his sins, nor to better his golf career, but to try and turn Tiger's heart back to Him. God loved Tiger enough to stop him from continuing to sin, even though that seems to knocked Tiger off from the top of his game. I sincerely wish Tiger all the best and I pray that he will climb back up to the top of the standings. I think he has great potential even now.

Tiger is still a very influential golfer, still drawing large crowds and viewers when he plays a tournament. To me, it feels like he's like Samson, tied to the pillars and looking for one last great deed, even if it kills him (Judges 16:28), except that Tiger doesn't seem to know that he needs to ask God for that help. I think that if Tiger wants to turn his career around, he needs to be more humble and to repent before God. That can't just be for show, either, but needs to be a real heart change. I think he could be like King David and turn his life around for the glory of God (and golf, in Tiger's case). In my opinion, if he repents and finds his freedom in Christ, then he could see real change not only in his life but also in his career. If he does manage to turn his life around, I think it would be the comeback story of the century.

CHRISTIAN WAY

Blessed is the one who does not
walk in step with the wicked
or stand in the way that sinners take
or sit in the company of mockers

Psalm 1:1

WHAT KIND OF PERSON ARE you when you're on the golf course? What personality traits come out? Are you the same person on the course that you are at home? What about at church? I've found that there is a worldly way to play golf and a Christian way. Competitive games like golf can bring out personality traits we didn't know we had. Golf and other games can also, sadly, cause us to commit sins like envy, pride, revenge, or worse. But when God calls us to give our whole lives to Him, that means everything, even our golf game. We need to behave the same way on the course as we do at church. We need to golf the Christian way.

What does it mean to golf in a worldly way versus the Christian way? I thought of a few of the sins that we can be tempted to commit on the golf course. The first is that we can be envious of other people. We can envy their skill, their clubs, even their clothes! But we need to be content with the good things that God has given us. The last of the Ten Commandments says, "You shall not covet your neighbour's house. You shall not covet your neighbour's wife, or his male or female servant, his ox or donkey, or anything that belongs to your neighbour." (Exodus 20:17) For golfers, we could say it a different way: "You shall not covet another golfer's swing. You shall not covet another golfer's coach, or his caddy, his clubs or cart, or anything that belongs to another golfer." God made each of us different and He gave each of us different blessings and different handicaps. We need to learn to be grateful for what we have been given and not to covet the blessings another golfer has *or* gloat over another golfer's handicaps.

That's one of the biggest sins we can be tempted towards on the course: the kind of pride that comes from gloating over another person's failures. We might see our opponent make a bad shot or get an unlucky bounce that costs them a stroke or two. How do we respond? Do we rejoice over their failure because it will mean that we have a chance to win? Or do we feel badly for them, knowing that we would feel badly in their place? That's how we can learn to look at it the Christian way: in your mind, reverse your positions. How would you feel if you were in your opponent's place, having just suffered an unlucky bounce? It works when your opponent gets lucky, too. You might be tempted to feel angry that they got a lucky break and you didn't. Instead of feeling angry or bitter, remember that luck goes both ways. It helps us to be humble. If that isn't enough incentive, read the words of Proverbs 24:17-18:

Do not gloat when your enemy falls;
when they stumble, do not let your heart rejoice,
or the Lord will see and disapprove
and turn his wrath away from them.

Your gloating might just be the thing that helps them win the match! In golf played the worldly way, your competitor's misery is your happiness, your opponent's fall is your rise in glory; but that is not the Christian way.

Have you ever found yourself critiquing someone else's swing in your mind—or even out loud? How do you feel when that person gets a great score? It's hard not to resent them for it. They have such an ugly swing and somehow they played such a good round! But remember Luke 6:37, when Jesus tells us, "Do not judge, and you will not be judged," and then in 6:41, "Why do you look at the speck of sawdust in your brother's eye and pay no attention to the plank in your own eye?" You can't see your own swing. For all you know, your swing might be just as ugly. It's better not to be in the habit of judging others, since you might be being judged in just the same way.

Sometimes we are tempted to golf in the worldly way because we see someone else doing it. What if we see our opponent cheating? How do we respond? It can be tempting to just throw the rules to the wind. "If he's going to cheat, then so am I!" we might think. But Paul reminds us in Romans 12:17, "Do not repay anyone evil for evil. Be careful to do what is right in the eyes of everyone." In other words, two wrongs don't make a right! You are responsible for your own behaviour. Cheating is a form of lying and that's not something that a Christian should make a practice of doing. So be careful to play golf "right" in the eyes of everyone.

What if there's a bet on the line, though? What then? First of all, I would recommend that you cut betting out of your game. It adds so much temptation to sin! In Romans 12:21, Paul wrote, "Do not be overcome by evil, but overcome evil with good." When we have a bet on the game and our opponent cheats, we might feel overcome by the evil and then we'll forget what Paul said previously about repaying evil for evil. We might also cheat because we are trying to win the bet. We are tempted to play the worldly way and not the Christian way.

If you really want to add some excitement to the game by betting, at least don't do it for cash. As Paul wrote in 1 Timothy 6:10, "For the love of money is a root of all kinds of evil. Some people, eager for money, have wandered from the faith and pierced themselves with many griefs." When we bet with money, it tempts us to commit all kinds of evil. We might even lose our faith over it! No golf bet is worth losing our faith. If you think about it, the Christian way of "betting" on a golf game could be even more upside down. What if the winner paid for the snacks and beverages at the end of the round? That way the loser doesn't have to suffer any more than he already has. It's a gracious, humble way of treating our friends with love. Our friendships are much more valuable than the money we might win if we bet on our golf round.

It is important to remember the value of our friendships when we're introducing a new golfer to the game, as well. We need to consider the new golfer's lack of skill. I've seen golfers who encouraged their friends to use the blue tee even when it was their first time on the course. It was only because they themselves wanted to start at the blue tee, maybe to show off. But then their friend—too new to the game to make a powerful drive—was very discouraged. They might not have played golf again. We need to be aware of the needs of others, even on the golf course. In 1 Corinthians, Paul talks about the dangers of eating meat prepared in pagan temples where they worshipped idols. He is concerned that new Christians might not understand that believers aren't under the control of these idols anymore and therefore might be tempted to worship the idols if they eat the meat. Paul writes, "Therefore, if what I eat causes my brother or sister to fall into sin, I will never eat meat again, so that I will not cause them to fall." (1 Corinthians 8:13) We need to have compassion for others, even on the golf course. If we're playing with a new golfer, we need to adjust our pace to suit their needs. We need to lead by example, not breaking the rules or cheating or being too competitive.

So far we've discussed the temptations of envy, pride, cheating, and betting. But we need to guard our hearts and our behaviour against even "little" sins. Have you ever found an abandoned ball on the course? Or maybe you've found good golf balls mixed in the bucket at the driving range? It's tempting to pocket them, isn't it? "What's the harm?" we might ask. "The owner obviously isn't coming back for it." The harm, though, is to our own souls. Every time we commit a sin—even one that seems small, like stealing one ball from the driving range—we are breaking God's heart. He has called Christians to be better than that so that our light will shine for everyone to see. In 1 Samuel 16:7, God says to Samuel, "The Lord does not look at the things people look at. People look at the outward appearance, but the Lord looks at the heart." We need to take care that nothing sinful gets into our hearts. God can see it even if no one else does.

We also need to be careful not to try to separate what is legal from what is right. What I mean is that sometimes we might argue that we're allowed to do something because it's legal. But that thing that we want to do might not be *right* even if it is legal. Our consciences will probably tell us when we're crossing that line. I think that the sporting world offers us a great comparison in the notion of sportsmanlike conduct. Sometimes it is unsportsmanlike to do something even when the rules of the game say that it's allowed. If we follow the rules so closely that we offend another player, then we are being unsportsmanlike. We are doing what is legal, but not what is right. Playing the Christian way means learning to tell the difference, just as living the Christian way means learning to listen to the Holy Spirit nudging our conscience towards what is right rather than just what is legal.

Golf is a competitive game. We can't take the competition out of the game completely. But we do have a choice to play the game in a worldly way or the Christian way. Of course we want to win. That goes without saying.

But we might have to adjust our understanding of what it means to win. Are we winning if we have to cheat? Are we winning when we rejoice over our opponent's failures? Are we winning if we lose our friendships over a few dollars? Are we winning when we make a new golfer feel bad about the game? The worldly way says that good guys finish last. If we follow the Christian way, we might not "win" every match. But when we have faith, that's when we are the real winners. The author of Hebrews writes, "And without faith it is impossible to please God, because anyone who comes to him must believe that he exists and that he rewards those who earnestly seek him." (Hebrews 11:6) When we believe in and follow God, he rewards us. Our real hope is in heaven. Paul writes the following to the church in Colossae:

> *We always thank God, the Father of our Lord Jesus Christ,*
> *when we pray for you, because we have heard of your faith*
> *in Christ Jesus and of the love you have for all God's people—*
> *the faith and love that spring from the hope stored up for*
> *you in heaven and about which you have already heard in*
> *the true message of the gospel that has come to you.*
>
> Colossians 1:3-6

He is thankful that these brothers and sisters in Christ have been living their faith, treating others well and following the Christian way, because they have set their hope on what is waiting for them in heaven. That's where we'll find our real winnings.

SCORECARD

AVE YOU EVER PLAYED "WHAT if" when you look back on your life? As in, "What if I had gone to trade school instead of university?" or "What if I had never started smoking?" or "What if I had invested in Coca-Cola instead of that dot-com start-up?" It's easy to imagine how wonderful our lives might have been *if only* we had made different decisions. But life is like a professional golf round: there are no mulligans. The bad choices and mistakes we made in the past stay with us, just as the good choices and lucky breaks still have an impact.

Imagine that we had golf scorecards for our lives. We'd have to divide up our expected lifetime into eighteen holes. So, say you expect to live to the ripe old age of 90. Each hole would then represent five years of your life. You can then look at your life so far and decide how well you've done. Say you're fifty right now. You're playing the tenth hole. You've rounded onto the back nine. Try scoring your previous holes. How did you do? One person might have been born into a family of millionaires. So they might score their first hole—their first five years of life—as an eagle. Lucky them! Another person might have spent their elementary school years goofing off and playing hooky. They have to admit they bogeyed that second hole—or worse. And so on.

Keep in mind that you need to keep score using a balance of worldly success and spiritual success. What I mean is that sometimes we can be succeeding wildly in the eyes of the world but completely neglecting our spiritual life. I don't think that makes for a great score, do you? I think often our successes are on a see-saw with worldly success and spiritual success on either end. As worldly success rises, our spiritual life falls, but when we find ourselves struggling in the eyes of the world, we might feel our spiritual life uplifted. As you score each "hole," keep these things in mind and remember that this exercise is only useful if you're being honest with yourself! Check out the example scorecard at the end of this chapter.

Using this life scorecard, we can look back on the "holes" we've already played and then try to make a plan for the rest of the holes. So if you're fifty and expect to live until you're ninety, you have eight holes left. Depending on how well you've scored yourself for the previous nine to ten holes, you might need to really up your game or maybe you'll need to keep grinding for par. Admittedly, in golf it's easy to determine how well you've been playing: it's just simple arithmetic. As we score our life and our walk with God, it's more about being critical and honest with ourselves. Don't beat yourself up about your past, but be honest about how things have gone so far. Just as in golf there is no perfect game, so too there is no perfect life. We all play bad holes. Dwelling on those past mistakes won't change them. Life and golf are not made for perfection. In both we will face serious challenges, hazards, and traps. Finally, when you've gotten an honest, non-judgmental measure of your life up until now, you can plan for what comes next.

Our goal, of course, is eternal life in Christ: that's our par. Anything less than par is our opportunity to be partners in building His Kingdom on earth now. We must not despair about our holes in the past. We now have an opportunity to do better and to refocus our lives on Jesus. Save your strokes. It's kind of like saving money so that you have an emergency fund for those times when life goes sideways. If you have the strokes to save, do it. Your next hole might not go as well as you hope since there are always going to be those challenges, hazards, and traps.

I also have some good news for you: the scorecard doesn't tell anyone *how* you got your score. In playing a hole, you might play a straightforward, easy par. Every time you hit the ball, it lands exactly where it should to make the next stroke easy. Or maybe you played an incredibly difficult hole. You nearly had to stand on your head to get the ball out of the rough and back onto the fairway, and then you made a forty-foot putt to secure that par. Either way, all you score on your card is par. There's no story on the card about how you got there. I find that comforting. It means that in the end, when I find myself in heaven, it doesn't matter how I got there. I always think of the thief hanging on the cross next to Jesus who was given the promise of paradise right before he died (Luke 23:40-43). He's the luckiest guy in history, scoring a hole-in-one on the last hole to make par for the round!

The other thing to remember is that we can't prewrite our scores. Our score isn't written until after we play the hole. That means that we can't predict success for ourselves *or* failure. Those of us with a glass-half-empty outlook on life need to remember that! Your score isn't prewritten and because of our hope in Christ, there is every reason to believe that even the worst score can be turned around. Our hope and faith give us the strength to believe that things can and will get better. With God, there is overwhelming opportunity for growth and change.

the old course

Date/Time	October 2015							H'cap		Strokes Rec'd		Par	SSS	Rating	Slope
Event	My Life											72	73	73.1	132
Player A	Stirling											72	71	71.4	129
Player B												76	76	75.6	138

Hole	Max. Time	Marker's Score	White Yards	Yellow Yards	Par	Men's S.I.	Player A	Player B	Pts +/-	Ladies' Yards	Par	Ladies' S.I.	Hole	Max Time	Marker's Score	White Yards	Yellow Yards	Par	Men's S.I.	Player A	Player B	Pts +/-	Ladies' Yards	Par	Ladies S.I.
1	0:13		376	355	4	10	2			339	4	12	10	2:09		340	311	4	15	4			296	4	13
2	0:27		411	395	4	6	3			375	5	14	11	2:18		174	164	3	7	6			150	3	17
3	0:40		370	337	4	16	6			321	4	8	12	2:30		316	304	4	3	7			304	4	3
4	0:54		419	411	4	8	3			401	5	6	13	2:45		418	388	4	11				377	5	11
5	1:11		514	514	5	2	8			454	5	2	14	3:02		530	523	5	1				487	5	1
6	1:24		374	360	4	12	6			325	4	10	15	3:16		414	391	4	9				369	4	5
7	1:37		359	349	4	4	5			335	4	4	16	3:29		381	345	4	13				325	4	9
8	1:45		166	154	3	14	2			145	3	18	17	3:44		455	436	4	5				426	5	7
9	1:57		347	289	4	18	4			261	4	16	18	3:57		357	361	4	17				342	4	15
Out	1:57		3336	3164	36		39			2956	38		In	2:00		3385	3223	36					3076	38	

Yardages on sprinkler heads are to the front edge of the green.
White numbers on front nine/red numbers on back nine.

Out	1:57	3336 3164 36 ... 2956 38
Total	3:57	6721 6387 72 ... 6032 76

Marker's Signature ....

Player's Signature ....

H'cap	
Nett Score	
Stableford Points or Par Result	

I filled out this sample scorecard from the St. Andrew's Old Course based on my life so far.

ACT 29

But the fruit of the Spirit is love, joy, peace, forbearance,
kindness, goodness, faithfulness, gentleness and self-control.
Against such things there is no law.

Galatians 5:22-23

I N GOLF, THE CLUBHOUSE—AND SPECIFICALLY its bar—is often called the
Nineteenth Hole. Obviously there isn't an actual nineteenth hole to play...
it's a metaphor. If you look in the Bible, you'll find that the Book of Acts
ends at chapter 28. I'd like you to imagine then, that there is a twenty-ninth
chapter of Acts. The secret is that this chapter is one you write yourself. Just
as golfers head into the "nineteenth hole" right after playing the eighteenth, I'd
encourage you to realize that Act 29 started when Acts 28 ended, and for each
of us it starts when our life in Christ begins. What kind of Act are we writing?
Is it heroic and filled with obedience? Or is it a tale of the struggle with sin and
the battle to overcome it? Probably it's a little of both.

If we want our Act 29 to fit in with the tales of the apostles and the early
Church, then it will help to cultivate the fruit of the Spirit in our lives. Practicing
those characteristics will help us to be obedient and humble servants. We have

to ask ourselves what we want out of life. Most of us, if we give in to what Paul calls our "flesh," will want nothing more than comfort and the satisfaction of our needs. A safe place to live, enough money to enjoy at least some luxuries, plenty of choice about what to eat, a person to love, lots of time to play golf... these are some of the things that we might centre our lives around. There's nothing wrong with these things at face value. But if that's all we're looking for in life, our Act 29 will be a pretty boring and uninspired story. We might think that it's a form of freedom to be able to choose these things, but I wonder how often we feel free to pursue physical comfort while we're still imprisoned by sin.

The spirit is willing but the flesh is weak (Matthew 26:41). We can be perfectly aware of how we *should* be living our lives, but it's so very easy just to let the desires of the flesh take over. It's like when we're golfing and we find ourselves tensing up. We know we need to stay relaxed if we want to swing well, but it can be hard to relax once that stiffness has crept in. It's especially hard when the game isn't going well. It's when we're worried about the difficult shot that we will be most tense. That tension in our muscles is like the tension in our lives as we fight to surrender everything to Jesus. We know that it will be easier to follow Him if we relax and let His Spirit lead us, but our desire for worldly things like money, power, and the other lusts of the flesh can overcome us, especially when life gets difficult. When our lives build up with that "tension," our ability to serve God is compromised. When a golfer is feeling the pressure to make a hard shot, there's a temptation to go back to old habits, to use a swing that's familiar, even if they know it's not a good swing. We do the same thing in our lives, don't we? When the going gets tough, we fall back into our old methods of coping, the things we did before we knew Jesus. We have to learn to trust that God will help us make a straight and true drive if we relax and let Him lead us. As it says in Proverbs 3:5, "Trust in the

Lord with all your heart and lean not on your own understanding."

I have to be honest, though. The struggle against sin and temptation and worldliness is one that we will all face over and over. Even Paul—a guy whom God chose to write Holy Scripture—struggled with sin. He tells the Christians in Rome, "For in my inner being I delight in God's law; but I see another law at work in me, waging war against the law of my mind and making me a prisoner of the law of sin at work within me. What a wretched man I am! Who will rescue me from this body that is subject to death?" (Romans 7:22-24) We don't hear testimonies like that in church very often. We often hear the stories of folks who hit rock bottom and then found Jesus and turned their life around. Those are very inspiring stories, to be sure! But sometimes we need to hear about the people who are keeping the faith, trusting in God and fighting the war against the law of sin inside of them, but who still find themselves in difficult circumstances. Instead of hearing the testimonies of people who have closed that chapter in their lives, we need to hear from people who are in the middle of it.

As we find ourselves in the middle of our Act 29, we might be wondering what the ultimate goal of this story really is. Where is the plot going? Or maybe we want to look at it as a sports game instead. In his book *Halftime*, Bob Buford describes the transition from a life pursuing success to the "second half" of life, pursuing the significance found in serving Christ. As I considered the metaphor of life as a football game, I felt like I'd moved past the first and second half and was well into overtime! I don't mean I'm into overtime in years on this earth, but just because I have faced so many struggles in my life so far. I'm sure his metaphor is very helpful to some people, but it didn't quite work for me. I began to think of my life more like a product with a warranty. Each of us has a limited warranty, and one day it will run out. But when we are born again as followers of Jesus (John 3:3), it's like taking out an extended warranty.

We won't find ourselves broken without anyone to fix us if we believe in Him. He ensures that we are covered.

The extended warranty that God provides will take us to our ultimate goal. What, then, is that goal? At the end of the Bible, in the last chapter of Revelation, Jesus promises that He is returning. Our ultimate goal is to join Him in the Holy City that He is going to bring when He unites heaven with earth. Everything in our Act 29 needs to be geared toward that goal. This is a book about golf and God, so let's think about our Act 29 in golfing terms. Every hole we play is like a battle against our own sin or against the temptations of worldliness. If every hole is a battle, then the entire round is the war. Our Act 29 could be thought of like a really long match play. It means that it's possible to lose a few holes and still win the match. We must strive to do our best on every hole, but also recognize that we might not be able to win every one. Our ultimate goal is to win the round. The most important "hole" we will play is the battle to keep our faith. The whole war depends on that.

I find it helps to ask myself what I want written on my tombstone or said at my funeral. I want to keep my eyes on the ultimate goal and live my life so that I achieve the best result: to live forever at God's side. I know it's tempting to look backward at our lives and be filled with regret. It's easy to be drawn into a day dream about how we might do things differently if we could only take a mulligan for that bad decision. But if we're honest with ourselves, I think we'd agree that we might not do anything differently. Not because we don't have regrets, but because of who we are and the circumstances we found ourselves in. If we play the same course twice on the same day, the outcomes will probably be very similar. If we lived our life twice, I think the results would be almost the same. As the saying goes, hindsight is 20/20. But when we're in the midst of our circumstances, we're going to be pretty short-sighted. It's only natural.

So we have a choice: do we look back on the story that has already been written, the game that's already been played, with regret and remorse? Or do we learn from it? When our lives are covered by Jesus' warranty, then we can look back at our past and see experiences and memories redeemed by repentance instead of regrets. And when we look ahead to the future, do we see only worries and concerns? If we listen to Jesus, then we can learn to see opportunities instead of worries. These opportunities are provided by God to help us become more like Him. When we trust in Him and let His Spirit lead, we can be assured of an Act 29 that will end well, secure in its ultimate goal, eternal life in the Kingdom of Heaven.

BIBLE VERSES

Taken from the New International Version (NIV)

DAY DREAMING

JOHN 4:24

God is spirit, and His worshipers must
worship in the Spirit and in truth.

WHAT IS GOLF?

PSALM 23:1-4

The Lord is my shepherd, I lack nothing.
  He makes me lie down in green pastures,
he leads me beside quiet waters,
  he refreshes my soul.
He guides me along the right paths
  for his name's sake.
Even though I walk
  through the darkest valley,
I will fear no evil,
  for you are with me;
your rod and your staff,
  they comfort me.

JOHN 21:15-17

When they had finished eating, Jesus said to Simon Peter,

"Simon son of John, do you love me more than these?"

"Yes, Lord," he said, "you know that I love you."

Jesus said, "Feed my lambs."

Again Jesus said, "Simon son of John, do you love me?"

He answered, "Yes, Lord, you know that I love you."

Jesus said, "Take care of my sheep."

The third time he said to him, "Simon son of John, do you love me?"

Peter was hurt because Jesus asked him the third time,

"Do you love me?" He said, "Lord, you know all things;

you know that I love you."

Jesus said, "Feed my sheep.

SIMILARITIES

PROVERBS 4:27

Do not turn to the right or the left;
  keep your foot from evil.

MATTHEW 26:41

Watch and pray so that you will not fall into temptation.
The spirit is willing, but the flesh is weak.

MATTHEW 5:38-39

You have heard that it was said, 'Eye for eye, and tooth for
tooth.' But I tell you, do not resist an evil person. If anyone slaps
you on the right cheek, turn to them the other cheek also."

ACTS 2:1-12

When the day of Pentecost came, they were all together in one place.
Suddenly a sound like the blowing of a violent wind came from heaven
and filled the whole house where they were sitting. They saw what
seemed to be tongues of fire that separated and came to rest on each

of them. All of them were filled with the Holy Spirit and began to
speak in other tongues as the Spirit enabled them.

Now there were staying in Jerusalem God-fearing Jews from every
nation under heaven. When they heard this sound, a crowd came
together in bewilderment, because each one heard their own language
being spoken. Utterly amazed, they asked: "Aren't all these who are
speaking Galileans? Then how is it that each of us hears them in
our native language? Parthians, Medes and Elamites; residents of
Mesopotamia, Judea and Cappadocia, Pontus and Asia, Phrygia and
Pamphylia, Egypt and the parts of Libya near Cyrene; visitors from
Rome (both Jews and converts to Judaism); Cretans and Arabs—we
hear them declaring the wonders of God in our own tongues!" Amazed
and perplexed, they asked one another, "What does this mean?"

TRINITY

1 CORINTHIANS 13:13

And now these three remain: faith, hope and
love. But the greatest of these is love.

ROMANS 5:3-4

Not only so, but we also glory in our sufferings, because
we know that suffering produces perseverance;
perseverance, character; and character, hope.

1 THESSALONIANS 5:16-18

Rejoice always, pray continually, give thanks in all
circumstances; for this is God's will for you in Christ Jesus.

EPHESIANS 4:4-6

There is one body and one Spirit, just as you were called to one
hope when you were called; one Lord, one faith, one baptism; one
God and Father of all, who is over all and through all and in all.

APPLICATION

MATTHEW 26:41

"Watch and pray so that you will not fall into temptation.
The spirit is willing, but the flesh is weak."

JAMES 2:17

In the same way, faith by itself, if it is not
accompanied by action, is dead.

1 JOHN 2:16

For everything in the world—the lust of the flesh, the lust of the eyes,
and the pride of life—comes not from the Father but from the world.

MATTHEW 14:29-31

"Come," he said.
Then Peter got down out of the boat, walked on the water and came
toward Jesus. But when he saw the wind, he was afraid and, beginning
to sink, cried out, "Lord, save me!"
Immediately Jesus reached out his hand and caught him.
"You of little faith," he said, "why did you doubt?"

PRACTICE

ROMANS 5:3-5

Not only so, but we also glory in our sufferings, because we
know that suffering produces perseverance; perseverance,
character; and character, hope. And hope does not put us
to shame, because God's love has been poured out into our
hearts through the Holy Spirit, who has been given to us.

MATTHEW 7:21

"Not everyone who says to me, 'Lord, Lord,' will
enter the kingdom of heaven, but only the one who

does the will of my Father who is in heaven.

1 CORINTHIANS 9:25-27

Everyone who competes in the games goes into strict training.
They do it to get a crown that will not last, but we do it to get a
crown that will last forever. Therefore I do not run like someone
running aimlessly; I do not fight like a boxer beating the air.
No, I strike a blow to my body and make it my slave so that
after I have preached to others, I myself will
not be disqualified for the prize.

JOSHUA 23:6

Be very strong; be careful to obey all that is written in the Book of
the Law of Moses, without turning aside to the right or to the left.

GALATIANS 6:7

Do not be deceived: God cannot be mocked. A man reaps what he sows.

JOB 23:10

But he knows the way that I take;
when he has tested me, I will come forth as gold.

SWING

EPHESIANS 6:13-17

Therefore put on the full armor of God, so that when the day of evil
comes, you may be able to stand your ground, and after you have done
everything, to stand. Stand firm then, with the belt of truth buckled
around your waist, with the breastplate of righteousness in place, and
with your feet fitted with the readiness that comes from the gospel of
peace. In addition to all this, take up the shield of faith, with which you
can extinguish all the flaming arrows of the evil one. Take the helmet
of salvation and the sword of the Spirit, which is the word of God.

MATTHEW 14:30

But when he saw the wind, he was afraid and,
beginning to sink, cried out, "Lord, save me!"

EPHESIANS 4:7

But to each one of us grace has been given as Christ apportioned it.

2 TIMOTHY 3:2-5

People will be lovers of themselves, lovers of money, boastful,
proud, abusive, disobedient to their parents, ungrateful, unholy,
without love, unforgiving, slanderous, without self-control, brutal,
not lovers of the good, treacherous, rash, conceited, lovers of
pleasure rather than lovers of God— having a form of godliness
but denying its power. Have nothing to do with such people.

GALATIANS 5:22-23

But the fruit of the Spirit is love, joy, peace, forbearance,
kindness, goodness, faithfulness, gentleness and self-
control. Against such things there is no law.

VISUALIZATION

HEBREWS 11:1

Now faith is confidence in what we hope for and
assurance about what we do not see.

JOHN 20:27-28

Then he said to Thomas, "Put your finger here; see my hands. Reach
out your hand and put it into my side. Stop doubting and believe."
Thomas said to him, "My Lord and my God!"

MATTHEW 14:28-31

"Lord, if it's you," Peter replied, "tell me to come to you on the water."

"Come," he said.

Then Peter got down out of the boat, walked on the water and came toward Jesus. But when he saw the wind, he was afraid and, beginning to sink, cried out, "Lord, save me!"

Immediately Jesus reached out his hand and caught him. "You of little faith," he said, "why did you doubt?"

GENESIS 19:15-26

With the coming of dawn, the angels urged Lot, saying, "Hurry! Take your wife and your two daughters who are here, or you will be swept away when the city is punished."

When he hesitated, the men grasped his hand and the hands of his wife and of his two daughters and led them safely out of the city, for the Lord was merciful to them. As soon as they had brought them out, one of them said, "Flee for your lives! Don't look back, and don't stop anywhere in the plain! Flee to the mountains or you will be swept away!"

But Lot said to them, "No, my lords, please! Your servant has found favor in your eyes, and you have shown great kindness to me in sparing my life. But I can't flee to the mountains; this disaster will overtake me, and I'll die. Look, here is a town near enough to run to, and it is small. Let me flee to it—it is very small, isn't it? Then my life will be spared."

He said to him, "Very well, I will grant this request too; I will not overthrow the town you speak of. But flee there quickly, because I cannot do anything until you reach it." (That is why the town was called Zoar.)

By the time Lot reached Zoar, the sun had risen over the land.

Then the Lord rained down burning sulfur on Sodom and
Gomorrah—from the Lord out of the heavens. Thus he
overthrew those cities and the entire plain, destroying all
those living in the cities—and also the vegetation in the land.
But Lot's wife looked back, and she became a pillar of salt.

MOMENT OF TRUTH

MATTHEW 16:15-16

"But what about you?" he asked. "Who do you say I am?"

Simon Peter answered, "You are the Messiah, the Son of the living God."

REVELATION 20:12-13

And I saw the dead, great and small, standing before the throne,
and books were opened. Another book was opened, which is the
book of life. The dead were judged according to what they had
done as recorded in the books. The sea gave up the dead that were
in it, and death and Hades gave up the dead that were in them,
and each person was judged according to what they had done.

GAME PLAN

MATTHEW 25:1-13

"At that time the kingdom of heaven will be like ten virgins who
took their lamps and went out to meet the bridegroom. Five of
them were foolish and five were wise. The foolish ones took their
lamps but did not take any oil with them. The wise ones, however,
took oil in jars along with their lamps. The bridegroom was a long
time in coming, and they all became drowsy and fell asleep.

"At midnight the cry rang out: 'Here's the
bridegroom! Come out to meet him!'

"Then all the virgins woke up and trimmed their lamps. The foolish ones said to the wise, 'Give us some of your oil; our lamps are going out.'

"'No,' they replied, 'there may not be enough for both us and you. Instead, go to those who sell oil and buy some for yourselves.'

"But while they were on their way to buy the oil, the bridegroom arrived. The virgins who were ready went in with him to the wedding banquet. And the door was shut.

"Later the others also came. 'Lord, Lord,' they said, 'open the door for us!'

"But he replied, 'Truly I tell you, I don't know you.'

"Therefore keep watch, because you do not know the day or the hour."

MATTHEW 6:33-34

But seek first his kingdom and his righteousness, and all these things will be given to you as well. Therefore do not worry about tomorrow, for tomorrow will worry about itself. Each day has enough trouble of its own.

INSTRUCTION

ROMANS 10:17

Consequently, faith comes from hearing the message, and the message is heard through the word about Christ.

1 CORINTHIANS 4:14-16

I am writing this not to shame you but to warn you as my dear children. Even if you had ten thousand guardians in Christ, you do not have many fathers, for in Christ Jesus I became your father through the gospel. Therefore I urge you to imitate me.

GOLF SCHOOL

PROVERBS 9:9-10

Instruct the wise and they will be wiser still;
   teach the righteous and they will add to their learning.

The fear of the Lord is the beginning of wisdom,
   and knowledge of the Holy One is understanding.

1 THESSALONIANS 5:19-22

Do not quench the Spirit. Do not treat prophecies with contempt
but test them all; hold on to what is good, reject every kind of evil.

FAITH

MATTHEW 14:30-32

But when he saw the wind, he was afraid and,
beginning to sink, cried out, "Lord, save me!"

Immediately Jesus reached out his hand and caught him.
"You of little faith," he said, "why did you doubt?"

And when they climbed into the boat, the wind died down.

HOPE

COLOSSIANS 1:3-6

We always thank God, the Father of our Lord Jesus Christ, when we
pray for you, because we have heard of your faith in Christ Jesus and of
the love you have for all God's people— the faith and love that spring
from the hope stored up for you in heaven and about which you have
already heard in the true message of the gospel that has come to you.

LOVE

1 CORINTHIANS 13:13

And now these three remain: faith, hope and
love. But the greatest of these is love.

1 THESSALONIANS 1:3

We remember before our God and Father your work
produced by faith, your labour prompted by love, and your
endurance inspired by hope in our Lord Jesus Christ.

HONESTY

2 TIMOTHY 4:7

I have fought the good fight, I have finished
the race, I have kept the faith.

1 SAMUEL 16:7

But the Lord said to Samuel, "Do not consider his appearance
or his height, for I have rejected him. The Lord does
not look at the things people look at. People look at the
outward appearance, but the Lord looks at the heart."

GRATITUDE

1 THESSALONIANS 5:16-18

Rejoice always, pray continually, give thanks in all
circumstances; for this is God's will for you in Christ Jesus.

GRACE

EPHESIANS 3:7

I became a servant of this gospel by the gift of God's
grace given me through the working of his power.

2 CORINTHIANS 12:9

But he said to me, "My grace is sufficient for you, for my power is made perfect in weakness." Therefore I will boast all the more gladly about my weaknesses, so that Christ's power may rest on me.

1 CORINTHIANS 15:10

But by the grace of God I am what I am, and his grace to me was not without effect. No, I worked harder than all of them—yet not I, but the grace of God that was with me.

ROMANS 6:1-2

What shall we say, then? Shall we go on sinning so that grace may increase? By no means! We are those who have died to sin; how can we live in it any longer?

HUMILITY

PHILIPPIANS 2:3-4

Do nothing out of selfish ambition or vain conceit. Rather, in humility value others above yourselves, not looking to your own interests but each of you to the interests of the others.

ROMANS 12:16

Live in harmony with one another. Do not be proud, but be willing to associate with people of low position. Do not be conceited.

PROVERBS 16:18

Pride goes before destruction,
a haughty spirit before a fall.

CRITIC

MATTHEW 7:1-5

"Do not judge, or you too will be judged. For in the same
way you judge others, you will be judged, and with the
measure you use, it will be measured to you.

"Why do you look at the speck of sawdust in your brother's
eye and pay no attention to the plank in your own eye? How
can you say to your brother, 'Let me take the speck out of your
eye,' when all the time there is a plank in your own eye? You
hypocrite, first take the plank out of your own eye, and then you
will see clearly to remove the speck from your brother's eye.

JAMES 2:14

What good is it, my brothers and sisters, if someone claims
to have faith but has no deeds? Can such faith save them?

100 EXCUSES

MATTHEW 6:19-21

Do not store up for yourselves treasures on earth, where moths
and vermin destroy, and where thieves break in and steal. But
store up for yourselves treasures in heaven, where moths and
vermin do not destroy, and where thieves do not break in and
steal. For where your treasure is, there your heart will be also.

QUITTING

ROMANS 8:38-39

For I am convinced that neither death nor life, neither angels nor
demons, neither the present nor the future, nor any powers, neither
height nor depth, nor anything else in all creation, will be able to
separate us from the love of God that is in Christ Jesus our Lord.

1 TIMOTHY 4:8

For physical training is of some value, but godliness has value for all things, holding promise for both the present life and the life to come.

1 SAMUEL 17

Now the Philistines gathered their forces for war and assembled at Sokoh in Judah. They pitched camp at Ephes Dammim, between Sokoh and Azekah. Saul and the Israelites assembled and camped in the Valley of Elah and drew up their battle line to meet the Philistines. The Philistines occupied one hill and the Israelites another, with the valley between them.

A champion named Goliath, who was from Gath, came out of the Philistine camp. His height was six cubits and a span. He had a bronze helmet on his head and wore a coat of scale armor of bronze weighing five thousand shekels; on his legs he wore bronze greaves, and a bronze javelin was slung on his back. His spear shaft was like a weaver's rod, and its iron point weighed six hundred shekels. His shield bearer went ahead of him.

Goliath stood and shouted to the ranks of Israel, "Why do you come out and line up for battle? Am I not a Philistine, and are you not the servants of Saul? Choose a man and have him come down to me. If he is able to fight and kill me, we will become your subjects; but if I overcome him and kill him, you will become our subjects and serve us." Then the Philistine said, "This day I defy the armies of Israel! Give me a man and let us fight each other." On hearing the Philistine's words, Saul and all the Israelites were dismayed and terrified.

Now David was the son of an Ephrathite named Jesse, who was from Bethlehem in Judah. Jesse had eight sons, and in Saul's time he was very old. Jesse's three oldest sons had followed Saul to the war: The firstborn was Eliab; the second, Abinadab; and the third, Shammah. David was the youngest. The three oldest followed Saul, but David went back and forth from Saul to tend his father's sheep at Bethlehem.

For forty days the Philistine came forward every morning and evening and took his stand.

Now Jesse said to his son David, "Take this ephah of roasted grain and these ten loaves of bread for your brothers and hurry to their camp. Take along these ten cheeses to the commander of their unit. See how your brothers are and bring back some assurance from them. They are with Saul and all the men of Israel in the Valley of Elah, fighting against the Philistines."

Early in the morning David left the flock in the care of a shepherd, loaded up and set out, as Jesse had directed. He reached the camp as the army was going out to its battle positions, shouting the war cry. Israel and the Philistines were drawing up their lines facing each other. David left his things with the keeper of supplies, ran to the battle lines and asked his brothers how they were. As he was talking with them, Goliath, the Philistine champion from Gath, stepped out from his lines and shouted his usual defiance, and David heard it. Whenever the Israelites saw the man, they all fled from him in great fear.

Now the Israelites had been saying, "Do you see how this man keeps coming out? He comes out to defy Israel. The king will give great wealth to the man who kills him. He will also give him his daughter in marriage and will exempt his family from taxes in Israel."

David asked the men standing near him, "What will be done for the man who kills this Philistine and removes this disgrace from Israel? Who is this uncircumcised Philistine that he should defy the armies of the living God?"

They repeated to him what they had been saying and told him, "This is what will be done for the man who kills him."

When Eliab, David's oldest brother, heard him speaking with the men, he burned with anger at him and asked, "Why have you come down here? And with whom did you leave those few sheep in the wilderness? I know how conceited you are and how wicked your heart is; you came down only to watch the battle."

"Now what have I done?" said David. "Can't I even speak?" He then turned away to someone else and brought up the same matter, and the men answered him as before. What David said was overheard and reported to Saul, and Saul sent for him.

David said to Saul, "Let no one lose heart on account of this Philistine; your servant will go and fight him."

Saul replied, "You are not able to go out against this Philistine and fight him; you are only a young man, and he has been a warrior from his youth."

But David said to Saul, "Your servant has been keeping his father's sheep. When a lion or a bear came and carried off a sheep from the flock, I went after it, struck it and rescued the sheep from its mouth. When it turned on me, I seized it by its hair, struck it and killed it. Your servant has killed both the lion and the bear; this uncircumcised Philistine will be like one of them, because he has defied the armies of the living God. The Lord who rescued me from the paw of the lion and the paw of the bear will rescue me from the hand of this Philistine."

Saul said to David, "Go, and the Lord be with you."

Then Saul dressed David in his own tunic. He put a
coat of armor on him and a bronze helmet on his head.
David fastened on his sword over the tunic and tried
walking around, because he was not used to them.

"I cannot go in these," he said to Saul, "because I am not
used to them." So he took them off. Then he took his staff
in his hand, chose five smooth stones from the stream,
put them in the pouch of his shepherd's bag and, with
his sling in his hand, approached the Philistine.

Meanwhile, the Philistine, with his shield bearer in front of him,
kept coming closer to David. He looked David over and saw that he
was little more than a boy, glowing with health and handsome, and he
despised him. He said to David, "Am I a dog, that you come at me with
sticks?" And the Philistine cursed David by his gods. "Come here,"
he said, "and I'll give your flesh to the birds and the wild animals!"

David said to the Philistine, "You come against me with sword and
spear and javelin, but I come against you in the name of the Lord
Almighty, the God of the armies of Israel, whom you have defied.
This day the Lord will deliver you into my hands, and I'll strike you
down and cut off your head. This very day I will give the carcasses of
the Philistine army to the birds and the wild animals, and the whole
world will know that there is a God in Israel. All those gathered here
will know that it is not by sword or spear that the Lord saves; for
the battle is the Lord's, and he will give all of you into our hands."

As the Philistine moved closer to attack him, David ran quickly
toward the battle line to meet him. Reaching into his bag and taking
out a stone, he slung it and struck the Philistine on the forehead. The
stone sank into his forehead, and he fell facedown on the ground.

So David triumphed over the Philistine with a
sling and a stone; without a sword in his hand he
struck down the Philistine and killed him.

David ran and stood over him. He took hold of the
Philistine's sword and drew it from the sheath. After
he killed him, he cut off his head with the sword.

When the Philistines saw that their hero was dead, they turned
and ran. Then the men of Israel and Judah surged forward with
a shout and pursued the Philistines to the entrance of Gath
and to the gates of Ekron. Their dead were strewn along the
Shaaraim road to Gath and Ekron. When the Israelites returned
from chasing the Philistines, they plundered their camp.

David took the Philistine's head and brought it to Jerusalem;
he put the Philistine's weapons in his own tent.

As Saul watched David going out to meet the Philistine, he said to
Abner, commander of the army, "Abner, whose son is that young man?"

Abner replied, "As surely as you live, Your Majesty, I don't know."

The king said, "Find out whose son this young man is."

As soon as David returned from killing the Philistine,
Abner took him and brought him before Saul, with
David still holding the Philistine's head.

"Whose son are you, young man?" Saul asked him.

David said, "I am the son of your servant Jesse of Bethlehem."

SIN

ROMANS 6:1-2

What shall we say, then? Shall we go on sinning so that
grace may increase? By no means! We are those who
have died to sin; how can we live in it any longer?

1 CORINTHIANS 9:23-27

Do you not know that in a race all the runners run, but only one
gets the prize? Run in such a way as to get the prize. Everyone
who competes in the games goes into strict training. They do it
to get a crown that will not last, but we do it to get a crown that
will last forever. Therefore I do not run like someone running
aimlessly; I do not fight like a boxer beating the air. No, I strike
a blow to my body and make it my slave so that after I have
preached to others, I myself will not be disqualified for the prize.

BREATHE

JOHN 16:33

"I have told you these things, so that in me you may
have peace. In this world you will have trouble. But
take heart! I have overcome the world."

MATTHEW 6:9-13

This, then, is how you should pray:

'Our Father in heaven,
hallowed be your name,
your kingdom come,
your will be done,
   on earth as it is in heaven.
Give us today our daily bread.

And forgive us our debts,
as we also have forgiven our debtors.
And lead us not into temptation,
but deliver us from the evil one.'

1 KINGS 19

Now Ahab told Jezebel everything Elijah had done and how he had
killed all the prophets with the sword. So Jezebel sent a messenger to
Elijah to say, "May the gods deal with me, be it ever so severely, if by
this time tomorrow I do not make your life like that of one of them."

Elijah was afraid and ran for his life. When he came to Beersheba
in Judah, he left his servant there, while he himself went a
day's journey into the wilderness. He came to a broom bush,
sat down under it and prayed that he might die. "I have had
enough, Lord," he said. "Take my life; I am no better than my
ancestors." Then he lay down under the bush and fell asleep.

All at once an angel touched him and said, "Get up and eat." He looked
around, and there by his head was some bread baked over hot coals,
and a jar of water. He ate and drank and then lay down again.

The angel of the Lord came back a second time and touched him
and said, "Get up and eat, for the journey is too much for you."
So he got up and ate and drank. Strengthened by that food, he
traveled forty days and forty nights until he reached Horeb, the
mountain of God. There he went into a cave and spent the night.

And the word of the Lord came to him:
"What are you doing here, Elijah?"

He replied, "I have been very zealous for the Lord God Almighty.
The Israelites have rejected your covenant, torn down your

altars, and put your prophets to death with the sword. I am
the only one left, and now they are trying to kill me too."

The Lord said, "Go out and stand on the mountain in the
presence of the Lord, for the Lord is about to pass by."

Then a great and powerful wind tore the mountains apart and
shattered the rocks before the Lord, but the Lord was not in
the wind. After the wind there was an earthquake, but the
Lord was not in the earthquake. After the earthquake came a
fire, but the Lord was not in the fire. And after the fire came a
gentle whisper. When Elijah heard it, he pulled his cloak over
his face and went out and stood at the mouth of the cave.

Then a voice said to him, "What are you doing here, Elijah?"

He replied, "I have been very zealous for the Lord God Almighty.
The Israelites have rejected your covenant, torn down your
altars, and put your prophets to death with the sword. I am
the only one left, and now they are trying to kill me too."

The Lord said to him, "Go back the way you came, and go to the
Desert of Damascus. When you get there, anoint Hazael king over
Aram. Also, anoint Jehu son of Nimshi king over Israel, and anoint
Elisha son of Shaphat from Abel Meholah to succeed you as prophet.
Jehu will put to death any who escape the sword of Hazael, and
Elisha will put to death any who escape the sword of Jehu. Yet
I reserve seven thousand in Israel—all whose knees have not
bowed down to Baal and whose mouths have not kissed him."

So Elijah went from there and found Elisha son of Shaphat. He was
plowing with twelve yoke of oxen, and he himself was driving the
twelfth pair. Elijah went up to him and threw his cloak around him.

Elisha then left his oxen and ran after Elijah. "Let me kiss my father and mother goodbye," he said, "and then I will come with you."

"Go back," Elijah replied. "What have I done to you?"

So Elisha left him and went back. He took his yoke of oxen and slaughtered them. He burned the plowing equipment to cook the meat and gave it to the people, and they ate. Then he set out to follow Elijah and became his servant.

IDOL

1 CORINTHIANS 12:15-20

Now if the foot should say, "Because I am not a hand, I do not belong to the body," it would not for that reason stop being part of the body. And if the ear should say, "Because I am not an eye, I do not belong to the body," it would not for that reason stop being part of the body. If the whole body were an eye, where would the sense of hearing be? If the whole body were an ear, where would the sense of smell be? But in fact God has placed the parts in the body, every one of them, just as he wanted them to be. If they were all one part, where would the body be? As it is, there are many parts, but one body.

POTTER & CLAY

ISAIAH 64:8

Yet you, Lord, are our Father.
　We are the clay, you are the potter;
　we are all the work of your hand.

ROMANS 9:21

Does not the potter have the right to make out of the same lump of clay some pottery for special purposes and some for common use?

IRON BYRON

DEUTERONOMY 32:4

He is the Rock, his works are perfect,
and all his ways are just.
A faithful God who does no wrong,
upright and just is he.

PROFESSIONAL VS. AMATEUR

MARK 10:42-45

Jesus called them together and said, "You know that those
who are regarded as rulers of the Gentiles lord it over them,
and their high officials exercise authority over them. Not so
with you. Instead, whoever wants to become great among you
must be your servant, and whoever wants to be first must be
slave of all. For even the Son of Man did not come to be served,
but to serve, and to give his life as a ransom for many."

PHILIPPIANS 2:6-11

Who, being in very nature God,
did not consider equality with God
something to be used to his own advantage;
rather, he made himself nothing
by taking the very nature of a servant,
being made in human likeness.
And being found in appearance as a man,
he humbled himself
by becoming obedient to death—
even death on a cross!

Therefore God exalted him to the highest place
and gave him the name that is above every name,

that at the name of Jesus every knee should bow,
in heaven and on earth and under the earth,
and every tongue acknowledge that Jesus Christ is Lord,
to the glory of God the Father.

RANGE FINDER

PROVERBS 21:31

The horse is made ready for the day of battle,
but victory rests with the Lord.

MULLIGAN

JOHN 3:3

Jesus replied, "Very truly I tell you, no one can see the
kingdom of God unless they are born again."

2 CORINTHIANS 5:17

Therefore, if anyone is in Christ, the new creation
has come: The old has gone, the new is here!

WHITE HOUSE

1 SAMUEL 16:7

But the Lord said to Samuel, "Do not consider his appearance
or his height, for I have rejected him. The Lord does
not look at the things people look at. People look at the
outward appearance, but the Lord looks at the heart."

PROVERBS 9:10

The fear of the Lord is the beginning of wisdom,
and knowledge of the Holy One is understanding.

SABBATH

MARK 2:27

Then he said to them, "The Sabbath was made
for man, not man for the Sabbath."

NOT FOR SALE

ACTS 8:17-21

Then Peter and John placed their hands on them,
and they received the Holy Spirit.

When Simon saw that the Spirit was given at the laying
on of the apostles' hands, he offered them money and
said, "Give me also this ability so that everyone on
whom I lay my hands may receive the Holy Spirit."

Peter answered: "May your money perish with you, because you
thought you could buy the gift of God with money! You have no part
or share in this ministry, because your heart is not right before God.

TECHNOLOGY

JOHN 14:6

Jesus answered, "I am the way and the truth and the life.
No one comes to the Father except through me."

ROMANS 6:1-2

What shall we say, then? Shall we go on sinning so that
grace may increase? By no means! We are those who
have died to sin; how can we live in it any longer?

ROMANS 12:2

Do not conform to the pattern of this world, but be transformed
by the renewing of your mind. Then you will be able to test and
approve what God's will is—his good, pleasing and perfect will.

BRAND NAME

1 SAMUEL 16:7

But the Lord said to Samuel, "Do not consider his appearance
or his height, for I have rejected him. The Lord does
not look at the things people look at. People look at the
outward appearance, but the Lord looks at the heart."

HANDICAP

1 CORINTHIANS 10:12

So, if you think you are standing firm, be careful that you don't fall!

PROVERBS 16:18

Pride goes before destruction,
a haughty spirit before a fall.

2 CORINTHIANS 12:9-10

But he said to me, "My grace is sufficient for you, for my power is made
perfect in weakness." Therefore I will boast all the more gladly about
my weaknesses, so that Christ's power may rest on me. That is why,
for Christ's sake, I delight in weaknesses, in insults, in hardships, in
persecutions, in difficulties. For when I am weak, then I am strong.

PLAYERS AND TOURS

EPHESIANS 4:7

But to each one of us grace has been given as Christ apportioned it.

PROVERBS 16:31

Gray hair is a crown of splendor;
it is attained in the way of righteousness.

2 SAMUEL 11

In the spring, at the time when kings go off to war, David sent Joab out with the king's men and the whole Israelite army. They destroyed the Ammonites and besieged Rabbah. But David remained in Jerusalem.

One evening David got up from his bed and walked around on the roof of the palace. From the roof he saw a woman bathing. The woman was very beautiful, and David sent someone to find out about her. The man said, "She is Bathsheba, the daughter of Eliam and the wife of Uriah the Hittite." Then David sent messengers to get her. She came to him, and he slept with her. (Now she was purifying herself from her monthly uncleanness.) Then she went back home. The woman conceived and sent word to David, saying, "I am pregnant."

So David sent this word to Joab: "Send me Uriah the Hittite." And Joab sent him to David. When Uriah came to him, David asked him how Joab was, how the soldiers were and how the war was going. Then David said to Uriah, "Go down to your house and wash your feet." So Uriah left the palace, and a gift from the king was sent after him. But Uriah slept at the entrance to the palace with all his master's servants and did not go down to his house.

David was told, "Uriah did not go home." So he asked Uriah, "Haven't you just come from a military campaign? Why didn't you go home?"

Uriah said to David, "The ark and Israel and Judah are staying in tents, and my commander Joab and my lord's men are camped in the open country. How could I go to my house to eat and drink and make love to my wife? As surely as you live, I will not do such a thing!"

Then David said to him, "Stay here one more day, and tomorrow I will send you back." So Uriah remained in Jerusalem that day and the next. At David's invitation, he ate and drank with him, and

David made him drunk. But in the evening Uriah went out to sleep on his mat among his master's servants; he did not go home.

In the morning David wrote a letter to Joab and sent it with Uriah. In it he wrote, "Put Uriah out in front where the fighting is fiercest. Then withdraw from him so he will be struck down and die."

So while Joab had the city under siege, he put Uriah at a place where he knew the strongest defenders were. When the men of the city came out and fought against Joab, some of the men in David's army fell; moreover, Uriah the Hittite died.

Joab sent David a full account of the battle. He instructed the messenger: "When you have finished giving the king this account of the battle, the king's anger may flare up, and he may ask you, 'Why did you get so close to the city to fight? Didn't you know they would shoot arrows from the wall? Who killed Abimelek son of Jerub-Besheth? Didn't a woman drop an upper millstone on him from the wall, so that he died in Thebez? Why did you get so close to the wall?' If he asks you this, then say to him, 'Moreover, your servant Uriah the Hittite is dead.'"

The messenger set out, and when he arrived he told David everything Joab had sent him to say. The messenger said to David, "The men overpowered us and came out against us in the open, but we drove them back to the entrance of the city gate. Then the archers shot arrows at your servants from the wall, and some of the king's men died. Moreover, your servant Uriah the Hittite is dead."

David told the messenger, "Say this to Joab: 'Don't let this upset you; the sword devours one as well as another. Press the attack against the city and destroy it.' Say this to encourage Joab."

When Uriah's wife heard that her husband was dead, she mourned for him. After the time of mourning was over, David had her brought to his house, and she became his wife and bore him a son. But the thing David had done displeased the Lord.

2 SAMUEL 12:1-13

The Lord sent Nathan to David. When he came to him, he said, "There were two men in a certain town, one rich and the other poor. The rich man had a very large number of sheep and cattle, but the poor man had nothing except one little ewe lamb he had bought. He raised it, and it grew up with him and his children. It shared his food, drank from his cup and even slept in his arms. It was like a daughter to him.

"Now a traveler came to the rich man, but the rich man refrained from taking one of his own sheep or cattle to prepare a meal for the traveler who had come to him. Instead, he took the ewe lamb that belonged to the poor man and prepared it for the one who had come to him."

David burned with anger against the man and said to Nathan, "As surely as the Lord lives, the man who did this must die! He must pay for that lamb four times over, because he did such a thing and had no pity."

Then Nathan said to David, "You are the man! This is what the Lord, the God of Israel, says: 'I anointed you king over Israel, and I delivered you from the hand of Saul. I gave your master's house to you, and your master's wives into your arms. I gave you all Israel and Judah. And if all this had been too little, I would have given you even more. Why did you despise the word of the Lord by doing what is evil in his eyes? You struck down Uriah the Hittite with the sword and took his wife to be your own. You killed him with the sword of the Ammonites. Now, therefore, the sword will never depart from your house, because you despised me and took the wife of Uriah the Hittite to be your own.'

"This is what the Lord says: 'Out of your own household I am going to bring calamity on you. Before your very eyes I will take your wives and give them to one who is close to you, and he will sleep with your wives in broad daylight. You did it in secret, but I will do this thing in broad daylight before all Israel.'"

Then David said to Nathan, "I have sinned against the Lord."

PROVERBS 16:18

Pride goes before destruction,
   a haughty spirit before a fall.

MATTHEW 10:17-31

Be on your guard; you will be handed over to the local councils and be flogged in the synagogues. On my account you will be brought before governors and kings as witnesses to them and to the Gentiles. But when they arrest you, do not worry about what to say or how to say it. At that time you will be given what to say, for it will not be you speaking, but the Spirit of your Father speaking through you.

"Brother will betray brother to death, and a father his child; children will rebel against their parents and have them put to death. You will be hated by everyone because of me, but the one who stands firm to the end will be saved. When you are persecuted in one place, flee to another. Truly I tell you, you will not finish going through the towns of Israel before the Son of Man comes.

"The student is not above the teacher, nor a servant above his master. It is enough for students to be like their teachers, and servants like their masters. If the head of the house has been called Beelzebul, how much more the members of his household!

"So do not be afraid of them, for there is nothing concealed that will not be disclosed, or hidden that will not be made known. What I tell you in the dark, speak in the daylight; what is whispered in your ear, proclaim from the roofs. Do not be afraid of those who kill the body but cannot kill the soul. Rather, be afraid of the One who can destroy both soul and body in hell. Are not two sparrows sold for a penny? Yet not one of them will fall to the ground outside your Father's care. And even the very hairs of your head are all numbered. So don't be afraid; you are worth more than many sparrows.

2 Corinthians 12:9

But he said to me, "My grace is sufficient for you, for my power is made perfect in weakness." Therefore I will boast all the more gladly about my weaknesses, so that Christ's power may rest on me.

Judges 16:28

Then Samson prayed to the Lord, "Sovereign Lord, remember me. Please, God, strengthen me just once more, and let me with one blow get revenge on the Philistines for my two eyes."

CHRISTIAN WAY

Psalm 1:1

Blessed is the one
    who does not walk in step with the wicked
or stand in the way that sinners take
    or sit in the company of mockers

Exodus 20:17

You shall not covet your neighbour's house. You shall not covet your neighbour's wife, or his male or female servant, his ox or donkey, or anything that belongs to your neighbour.

PROVERBS 24:17-18

Do not gloat when your enemy falls;
  when they stumble, do not let your heart rejoice,
or the Lord will see and disapprove
  and turn his wrath away from them.

LUKE 6:37

Do not judge, and you will not be judged. Do not condemn, and
you will not be condemned. Forgive, and you will be forgiven.

LUKE 6:41

Why do you look at the speck of sawdust in your brother's
eye and pay no attention to the plank in your own eye?

ROMANS 12:17

Do not repay anyone evil for evil. Be careful to
do what is right in the eyes of everyone.

ROMANS 12:21

Do not be overcome by evil, but overcome evil with good.

1 TIMOTHY 6:10

For the love of money is a root of all kinds of evil. Some
people, eager for money, have wandered from the
faith and pierced themselves with many griefs.

1 CORINTHIANS 8:13

Therefore, if what I eat causes my brother or sister to fall into sin,
I will never eat meat again, so that I will not cause them to fall.

1 Samuel 16:7

But the Lord said to Samuel, "Do not consider his appearance
or his height, for I have rejected him. The Lord does
not look at the things people look at. People look at the
outward appearance, but the Lord looks at the heart."

Hebrews 11:6

And without faith it is impossible to please God, because
anyone who comes to him must believe that he exists
and that he rewards those who earnestly seek him.

Colossians 1:3-6

We always thank God, the Father of our Lord Jesus Christ, when we
pray for you, because we have heard of your faith in Christ Jesus and of
the love you have for all God's people— the faith and love that spring
from the hope stored up for you in heaven and about which you have
already heard in the true message of the gospel that has come to you.

SCORECARD

Luke 23:40-43

But the other criminal rebuked him. "Don't you fear God,"
he said, "since you are under the same sentence? We
are punished justly, for we are getting what our deeds
deserve. But this man has done nothing wrong."

Then he said, "Jesus, remember me when
you come into your kingdom."

Jesus answered him, "Truly I tell you, today
you will be with me in paradise."

ACT 29

GALATIANS 5:22-23

But the fruit of the Spirit is love, joy, peace, forbearance, kindness, goodness, faithfulness, gentleness and self-control. Against such things there is no law.

MATTHEW 26:41

Watch and pray so that you will not fall into temptation. The spirit is willing, but the flesh is weak.

PROVERBS 3:5

Trust in the Lord with all your heart
   and lean not on your own understanding

ROMANS 7:22-24

For in my inner being I delight in God's law; but I see another law at work in me, waging war against the law of my mind and making me a prisoner of the law of sin at work within me. What a wretched man I am! Who will rescue me from this body that is subject to death?

Made in the USA
Columbia, SC
03 November 2020